Boat Handling

Boat Handling

By the Editors of
TIME-LIFE BOOKS

The
TIME-LIFE Library of Boating

TIME-LIFE BOOKS, NEW YORK

TIME-LIFE BOOKS

Founder: Henry R. Luce 1898-1967

Editor-in-Chief: Hedley Donovan
Chairman of the Board: Andrew Heiskell
President: James R. Shepley
Group Vice President: Rhett Austell

Vice Chairman: Roy E. Larsen

Managing Editor: Jerry Korn
Assistant Managing Editors: Ezra Bowen,
David Maness, Martin Mann, A. B. C. Whipple

Planning Director: Oliver E. Allen
Art Director: Sheldon Cotler
Chief of Research: Beatrice T. Dobie
Director of Photography: Melvin L. Scott
Senior Text Editor: Diana Hirsh
Assistant Art Director: Arnold C. Holeywell
Assistant Chief of Research: Myra Mangan

Publisher: Joan D. Manley
General Manager: John D. McSweeney
Business Manager: Nicholas J. C. Ingleton
Sales Director: Carl G. Jaeger
Promotion Director: Paul R. Stewart
Public Relations Director: Nicholas Benton

The TIME-LIFE Library of Boating

Series Editor: Harvey B. Loomis

Editorial staff for Boat Handling:
Text Editors: Philip W. Payne, Bryce S. Walker
Picture Editors: Catherine Ireys, Robert G. Mason
Designer: Bruce Blair
Assistant Designers: James Eisenman, Elaine Zeitsoff
Staff Writers: Richard Cravens, Lee Hassig,
Susan Hillaby, Kirk Landers, Don Nelson,
Richard Oulahan
Chief Researcher: Nancy Shuker
Researchers: Jane Colihan, Holly Evarts,
Stuart Gannes, James B. Murphy, Joyce Pelto,
Janice Pikey, Janet Zich
Design Assistant: Sanae Yamazaki
Editorial Assistant: Cecily Gemmell

Editorial Production
Production Editor: Douglas B. Graham
Assistant Production Editors: Gennaro C. Esposito,
Feliciano Madrid
Quality Director: Robert L. Young
Assistant Quality Director: James J. Cox
Copy Staff: Eleanore W. Karsten (chief),
Eleanor Van Bellingham, Mary Ellen Slate,
Florence Keith, Pearl Sverdlin
Picture Department: Dolores A. Littles,
Carolyn Turman
Traffic: Carmen McLellan

The Cover: Raising a welter of foam, the skipper of a nimble 28-foot cruiser tests his craft's rough-water handling qualities by deliberately cutting across the curling wake of another vessel.

The Consultants: Carleton Mitchell has logged more than 50 years as a racing skipper and cruising man, under sail and power, and is the author of seven books and scores of articles on nautical matters.

John D. Atkin is a yacht designer and professional surveyor as well as Commodore of the Huntington Cruising Club of Darien, Connecticut.

G. James Lippmann, a naval architect, is the executive director of the American Boat and Yacht Council.

Conrad Miller, a technical editor of *Motor Boating & Sailing,* and a consultant to the Westlawn School of Yacht Design, is author of *Small Boat Engines* and other books on marine technology.

William Munro, a powerboatman with more than 30 years of experience, is a photographer and author of many articles, for *Motorboat* magazine and other boating publications.

John Rousmaniere, a small-boat sailor and veteran ocean racer, is the West Coast editor of *Yachting* magazine.

Owen C. Torrey Jr. is chief designer at Charles Ulmer, Inc., sailmakers.

Valuable assistance was given by the following departments and individuals of Time Inc.: Editorial Production, Norman Airey; Library, Benjamin Lightman, Lester Annenberg; Picture Collection, Doris O'Neil; Photographic Laboratory, George Karas; TIME-LIFE News Service, Murray J. Gart; Correspondent Molly Schaefer (Detroit).

Contents

The Robust Art of Boat Handling

The Robust Art of Boat Handling

By Norris D. Hoyt

For some people the joy of boating comes from simply being out on the open water on a clear day, with the seagulls wheeling and crying. But harmony with the elements is only the beginning of boating's rewards. For the true boatman, final satisfaction comes with the harmony of thought and action, of anticipation and response, that makes his craft an extension of his will. The expert boat handler, whether in close quarters at a dock or clawing off a lee shore in half a gale, takes special pleasure in quickly sizing up his situation and knowing to an inch the extent of his boat's abilities to respond.

Competence in handling even small boats is infinitely satisfying in itself —and this same competence, applied to larger craft, has at the highest level of performance won international trophies, saved lives and even saved nations. In this latter category, the maneuvers of Horatio Nelson at the Battle of Cape St. Vincent provide a stunning example of superior and decisive boat handling. In the winter of 1797, Nelson was off southern Portugal, commanding one of 15 ships under Admiral Sir John Jervis. England was faltering in its war against France, and Jervis had orders to keep a 27-ship Spanish fleet from joining with the French. Jervis lay in wait off Cape St. Vincent and on Valentine's Day the Spaniards arrived, straggling along in two groups. Boldly, Jervis led his ships in single file through the gap, intending to keep the Spaniards divided and then turn and attack them piecemeal.

Nelson, near the end of the British line, saw that the plan would fail because the British ships could not come about fast enough to press their advantage. But knowing the capabilities of his own ship, the 74-gun *Captain*, Nelson realized that he had just time to intercept one portion of the divided Spanish fleet. He changed course, broke from the line and engaged the thoroughly astonished Spaniards. His maneuver threw them into such confusion that two of them collided and locked in a tangle of spars and cordage. Spanish gunners had by now shot away *Captain*'s rigging, but Nelson, still handling her superbly, used the last of his ship's momentum to come alongside the two disabled Spaniards; sword in hand, he boarded and captured them in quick succession. The rest of the English fleet immediately followed up Nelson's initiative. Two more Spaniards capitulated and the rest fled to Cadiz where Jervis bottled them up. Expert boat handling won the day, brought Nelson a knighthood—and may even have saved England.

Anyone over the age of four is ready to begin the learning process for such consummate boat handling. Most officers in Nelson's time first went to sea at the age of 12 or so. I made my first voyage at a slightly younger age—and on a somewhat more modest scale—when I crossed a small pond in a large box. Since then I have sailed 20 times across the Atlantic, motored across twice, trailered a two-ton auxiliary the length and breadth of the United States, and driven outboards, motor cruisers, PT boats and a destroyer. And to this day, I envy the skills of many boatmen and imitate their techniques.

Narragansett Bay in Rhode Island, where I sail much of the year, is home water for hundreds of Azorean-born boatmen who scrape shellfish from the bay floor with long rakes. They travel in heavy, flat-bottomed 20-foot skiffs powered by 40-horse outboards. Planing over the bay's calm waters, the fishermen stand easily in their boats, steering from amidships and controlling their speed by means of long pipe handles attached to their motors. When running before the wind in a rising sea—difficult conditions for the average powerboatman—these experts merely move back to let their bows lift a little while they subtly alter their speed to catch each overtaking wave just right. Then they ride the waves like surfers, shooting along just before each crest but never going so fast as to shove a boat's snout into the wave ahead.

I saw one of these wave riders at his very best one afternoon when I was steaming into Newport aboard a Coast Guard cutter that was traveling at about 18 knots. As our wake crested under his quarter, he swung parallel to us, climbed on the face of our wave and, matching its speed with precision, rode it for almost two fuel-saving miles, his teeth shining in pure white pleasure under his ferocious moustache.

Like Lord Nelson, that expert Azorean boat handler had started young and probably in a rowboat, as practically everybody does. A rowboat is a perfect place for a novice to start learning, to begin to sense that all-important rhythm every boat seems to ask for in its relationship to wind and water. The aspirant boatman should learn the right way to row—catching the water cleanly with his oar blades, bringing his back into the middle of the pull, easing off and snapping the oar free with a feather of the wrists, then leaning forward to catch again, lifting the boat along before it loses its run. A good oarsman never hurries the sequence. He feels the tempo of a harbor chop, anticipates each wave and waits to drive over it, rather than smashing into a crest and soaking his passengers. The skilled oarsman handles his boat easily and safely, with a rhythm as elegant as a dancer's.

Anticipation, balance and a sense of the boat's natural rhythm are as important to the powerboatman as to the rower, and practice is the key to learning them. The novice skipper of a small outboard boat, for example, can learn a lot about the behavior of his craft simply by asking his passengers to shift their weight, first forward and then aft. Or he can get the feel of his boat's maneuverability by dropping a flotation cushion overboard and circling around to pick it up; or by backing slowly in a crosswind, or by cutting his engine and shooting up to a dock without power. After a while the skipper will know the speed at which his craft is most comfortable in any kind of a sea. Too fast, and the waves turn the ride into a series of bone-jarring crashes, like riding a jalopy across a plowed field; too slow, and the result is a vicious rocking that scrambles together gear, passengers and lunch.

Those same senses of rhythm and of anticipation apply even to the somewhat less joyous task of towing a boat on a trailer. A change in road surface, like a change in wave action, can set a trailered boat oscillating left and right, and can seriously affect the car's steering. The best solution is to slow down, for it is easy to overcompensate for yawing, and at high speeds the result can be catastrophic. Practice—and common sense—make the chore easier.

For me, one of the most memorable demonstrations of boat mastery was put on by a 10-year-old fisherman I once saw trolling the shoreline of a lake in a rubber boat with a two-horsepower outboard. The motor, locked in a straight-ahead position, muttered gently to itself, and the fisherman, concentrating on the line trailing out from his rod tip, sat well forward, not touching the motor. As the boat drew its wake across the mirror of the evening lake, he shifted his weight just a little to one side or the other, shoreward or offshore —and the boat wove a perfect parallel to every curve of the beach. I know that he can ride his bike with both hands in his pockets, too.

I have seen other youngsters equally skilled, and have experienced the great satisfaction of teaching some of them. At a sailing class I supervised for small boys, we had weekly games of tennis-ball tag among the skippers of a small fleet of tiny sailing prams. Whoever started out as "it" tried to hit the skipper of another boat with a tennis ball. If he missed, he had to sail to the ball, scoop it out of the water and let fly again; if he scored, his target became "it." Collisions counted against the offenders. The maneuvering was frenetic, and the young skippers quickly learned what their boats could do and how to make them do it. I like to think it is not entirely coincidence that three of those lads later sailed on *Intrepid* in a successful defense of the America's Cup, or that virtually all of them have done themselves credit in the Newport to Bermuda ocean-racing classic.

Skills honed by constant practice in small boats always carry over into the handling of bigger ones. The experience of retired Navy Captain E. Arthur Shuman Jr., of Marblehead, Massachusetts, is a classic example. As a small boy he started sailing in dinghys, later moving up through 18-foot and 28-foot sail-

The author, behind the wheel of his 41-foot Carib sloop, Telltale 2, has been an enthusiastic sailor since childhood. After commanding a PT boat during World War II, he taught sailing—among other things—for over 20 years at St. George's School in Newport, Rhode Island. His cruising and racing experiences include crossing the Atlantic under both power and sail. Hoyt has written a guide, Seamanship, as well as many articles for sport and yachting magazines.

boats. Shuman had advanced to ocean racing in 70-footers by the time he was called to active duty in World War II by the Navy. There, as an ensign he again started small—with patrol craft—and moved up eventually to the 377-foot destroyer *Waldron*.

One day in 1946, soon after the war's end, he dramatically demonstrated his boat handling skills, first acquired on a tiny dinghy but applicable all the way up the boating scale. Coming in to dock his destroyer at Boston's Charlestown navy yard, Shuman found he had to squeeze his vessel between two ships—one of them a mammoth cruiser—and then jockey it to a landing between the cruiser's bow and a dry dock. He had only about 10 feet of leeway all around and stood a handsome chance of ramming the cruiser or of coming in too fast and slamming the *Waldron* right into the dry dock's bulkhead. Nevertheless he decided to dock without the aid of a tug or harbor pilot. And did it, flawlessly. Slipping past the cruiser, he cut his starboard engine, signaled the engine room for reverse on the port screw and slid the *Waldron's* 2,200 tons precisely alongside the dock. Later the Navy posted Shuman—by then Commander—to the Naval Academy as head of a sailing and small-boat program that still turns out the world's best naval ship handlers.

Nobody, unless he has to, docks a large ocean liner in the offhand way that former Commander Shuman parked his destroyer. But sometimes a liner captain has to. During a New York tug strike, Captain Frederick G. Watts of the Cunard Line used boat handling skills acquired over 41 years to put all 1,031 feet of the *Queen Elizabeth* into a dock at right angles to the Hudson River's current in 20 knots of wind. The feat probably gave Lloyd's of London cold chills; but it also gave Captain Watts the thrill that every skipper experiences from bringing off a neat bit of boat handling in difficult circumstances before an appreciative audience.

The sailor's equivalent of docking a motorboat is making his mooring—not too hard on a small sailboat because it is light and loses speed rapidly. But a large sailboat has tons of lead on its keel, has no brakes and coasts forever. Once, on a gusty afternoon, a commodore of the prestigious New York Yacht Club made seven unsuccessful attempts to pick up his mooring in crowded Newport Harbor. In his 73-foot craft he boiled through other moored boats, rounded up into the wind and came coasting toward his mooring, mainsail flogging in the wind. Each time the wind either rose in a gust and stalled him short or dropped so suddenly that he swept by in the calm.

His wife sensibly suggested that he lower his sails and use the boat's highly competent diesel engine. Stony silence greeted this feminine practicality. On the eighth try, the wind and the commodore reached an accommodation, and one crew member leaned over the bow and picked up the mooring as the rest of us dropped and furled the sails. The commodore sat down with a "mission accomplished" air. He had the full approval of every sailing man in the harbor: A sailor, sir, shoots his mooring under sail.

Part of the joy of boat handling is that even a failure—or seven failures—becomes a positive part of the process of experience building, of getting to know just what you and your boat can do in varying circumstances. Study and observation are helpful parts of the process, too—watching others use their boat handling skills can add significantly to your own mastery of the art.

In heavy weather on a Block Island race I once watched a fine racing skipper named Bill Snaith drive his 47-foot yawl *Figaro* to windward. Whereas helmsmen on other boats in the race were coming off wave crests at seven and a half knots, slamming into the shoulder of the next sea and slowing to six knots, Bill treated his boat like a lady, sensing her every need. Delicately anticipating each wave, he eased off across the crest, met the next oncoming sea obliquely, then lifted with the sea and eased again. His gentling took most of the slam and half the slowing out of the impact.

A few years later when I was sailing in the 46-foot sloop *Cyane* in the 1960 Bermuda race, we were hit on the nose by a gale just after crossing the Gulf Stream. While other boats were driving into the steep seas, we were working through them, using the same technique Snaith had employed so effectively on *Figaro. Cyane* passed 32 competitors in one four-hour period.

Observation and experience—and anticipation—should build in a boatman not only confidence but also caution. A beginning boat handler should heed the instinctive warnings that his common sense will trigger to avoid situations beyond his skill or the boat's abilities. He will stay out of heavy maritime traffic until he knows and can apply the Rules of the Road. When lost he will stop and perhaps even drop anchor rather than blunder on into unseen dangers. He will avoid entering a wave-swept inlet or crossing a breaking bar in a sailboat or in a slow, heavy powerboat. Instead, he will idle around outside until the sea dies or high tide puts adequate water between his keel and the bar. With experience and with a boat that can go faster than the waves, a boatman can learn to climb on the back of a cresting sea and ride it right down a channel full of combers—just the way that Azorean fisherman rode our wake into Narragansett Bay.

When you have mastered the basic skills, you can extend yourself to the limit with the kind of all-out physical challenge that boat handling can provide. Try driving a twin-engined V-bottom powerboat through a quartering sea at a good clip; absolute attention, fast hands and a strong back are what you need to lay a straight wake. Or exercise every muscle from your ears to your toes while rocketing along in a snarling outboard racer around the buoys of a competition course, as more and more adventurous powerboatmen are doing. Hike out from a sailing dinghy, your shoulders riding inches off the water as long as your stomach muscles hold out. No matter where you finish, you will feel you've won when you stop.

Enjoy, like a true child of the 20th Century, the intricacies of equipment. A boat—any boat—is a complex instrument compounded of hull shape, motive power and guidance mechanism. As you progress through the years and your skill in boat handling grows, your equipment—whether it is in the area of increased horsepower or more advanced electronic controls or highly specialized sails—becomes more sophisticated, more of a challenge to master. New kinds of sails, for example, are invented every year, like the so-called "Confederate staysail," an elongated sail that one skipper devised to set in the empty space beneath his main boom. You may want to try a bit of innovating yourself. Consider the difficulty of backing a shallow-draft boat into a narrow slip in a crosswind. One boatman tried using a centerboard on the bow of his powerboat to keep the head of his vessel from drifting sideways in these circumstances. The device was not entirely successful, but perhaps you will come up with something better.

You may even save a life by instant anticipation in a crisis and expert application of boat handling skills. My distant cousin, C. Sherman Hoyt, a preeminent racing helmsman of a few decades ago, did just that on a stormy day during the 1935 transatlantic race to Norway. He was steering the 70-foot ketch *Vamarie* when, during a sail change, the spinnaker pole slipped, stunned one of the crewmen and knocked him overboard. Hoyt shot the boat into the wind with all sails still set. As the back-winded spinnaker stopped the boat, he skillfully steered it backward while the man forward worked to make the sails draw; then, with one quick tack Hoyt rounded the boat up next to the floating man, who was quickly scooped aboard. Any other maneuver, or a 10-second lag in making the only right one, would have doomed the man. A lifetime of sailing small and large boats, day and night, had equipped Hoyt to make the right move instantly.

As long as you live with boats, the challenges and the joys of problem solving never end. The joys become more intense as you attack the problems with your growing arsenal of techniques. Start with the assurance that you can translate the principles of boat handling into experience. Try out some of these techniques on a clear day, with the seagulls wheeling, when nobody is looking at you. Work at them until you have confidence in your own skills and judgment. For confidence is the mother of joy.

1 Part of the excitement of boating is the sense of anticipation that wells up as the yachtsman readies his boat to go out on the water. The preparations may involve stepping onto the deck of a 60-foot racing sloop and bending on hundreds of square feet of expensively cut Dacron sails. Getting ready may be as simple as a trip to the gas station to fill up an outboard's portable fuel tank. Or it may entail the most basic boating situation of all—climbing into a rowboat and ferrying away from the dry land, as the man at left is doing, to reach a vessel moored in the middle of a harbor. But it makes no difference whether the craft is a six-foot dinghy or a transoceanic yacht—the success of its voyage will depend

HEADING OUT ON THE WATER

on the preliminary steps the skipper should take to ensure the safety and well-being of both his boat and its passengers.

The skipper's first preparatory act should be to check the weather. A cardinal rule of boating is that when storm warnings are out, the boat stays in. Boating forecasts often are printed in local newspapers or broadcast by local radio stations—or they may be obtained by phoning the Coast Guard. Moreover, most yacht clubs and marinas fly red pennants when the wind is likely to gust to 30 knots or more, as an advisory to small craft to stay home.

When the mariner is satisfied that the elements are kindly, he should consider the soundness of his boat and its equipment. Do his running lights work? Is his fire extinguisher full and functioning? Does he have a life preserver for each passenger as the law requires? Are these items and all the other gear he needs aboard properly stowed where they will stay in place if a rising sea rocks the boat? Even more important, is he sure that he can get at them in a hurry when needed? Preservers that are inaccessibly squirreled away in the forepeak will save no lives. The skipper should pump out any water that has seeped into the bilge since the last trip and should check for leaks if the bilges seem too full. He might also spend a moment swabbing the deck; dirt and oil spills are slippery and unseamanlike, and they can soil life preservers, sails and his passengers' best yachting clothes.

A head count of the passengers is an essential part of the starting ritual; too many people means an uncomfortable or downright hazardous ride. On motor-powered craft up to 20 feet long, the manufacturer is required to install a plate indicating the boat's maximum weight capacity, which helps the boatman determine the number of occupants the boat can safely carry; on sailboats the size of the crew depends upon the craft's design. A 19-foot racer might be built for only two or three crewmen; a cruiser of the same length could easily haul six or more. Regardless of manufacturer's labels or skipper's judgment, however, the Coast Guard, and some state or local authorities may turn back to shore any boat they consider to be overloaded.

For both safety and comfort, the skipper should brief passengers on certain seagoing rules of conduct. Three basic dicta are: no smoking while the boat is being fueled; no standing up on small craft that could tip over easily; and all children and weak swimmers must don life jackets as soon as they step aboard. It is also a good idea for the skipper to insist that passengers wear long-sleeved shirts and long trousers to protect sensitive skin on bright, sunny days. And, since temperatures can drop suddenly on the water, spare jackets or sweaters are recommended gear.

In addition, the helmsman should be certain there is a competent backup skipper aboard in case the skipper himself falls overboard or becomes disabled. Finally, before the boat sets off, someone on shore should be told where it is going and how long it will be gone—leaving word to sound the alarm if the vessel is delayed in getting back to the dock.

A day afloat begins with getting aboard. The oarsman at left is pulling steadily away from the dock and out into the harbor, heading for the mooring where his vessel awaits him.

Powerboat Preparations

When a powerboat skipper gets ready to take his craft for a spin, the first thing he should do is check out the equipment needed for the trip. Much of the equipment, shown with the typical 19-foot runabout at right, is required by law. This mandatory gear includes a fire extinguisher, a horn or a whistle, and a Coast Guard-approved life jacket for each person on board—plus at least one throwable lifesaving device. Since the fuel tanks in the boat shown here are kept in sheltered compartments aft, the compartments are vented, as required, by cowled ducts to carry off gas vapors. For going out after dark, the running-light fitting at the bow shows red to port and green to starboard; the staff on the starboard quarter has a white light at its top.

Beyond these legal necessities, the prudent skipper also carries gear needed to meet any number of manual boat handling situations—as well as occasional breakdowns. Foremost among these articles is a bilge pump for taking out the water shipped aboard in rough weather. There should also be an anchor, ready to be dropped over the side either at some planned destination, or as a safety measure if the boat should start drifting into trouble. Another key item is the owner's manual for the engine, which provides instructions on the care and handling of the power plant; the manual should be accompanied by a tool kit for minor repairs. If the motor fails, two useful items are a paddle and extra line—perhaps a spare docking line—that could be used for a tow. Fenders made of soft rubber or plastic are carried to protect the hull from impact with the dock or other boats.

Fuel Safety Check List

The skipper should observe the following safety rules at each fueling.
1. Fill portable tanks off the boat.
2. When fueling fixed tanks, close doors and hatches to keep fumes from collecting in the boat's interior.
3. Keep the fire extinguisher handy.
4. Permit no smoking.
5. Do not operate electrical equipment.
6. Keep the gasoline nozzle in contact with the tank aperture at all times to prevent static sparks.
7. Wipe up spills immediately.
8. Stop fueling before the gas level reaches the top, and replace the cap tightly.
9. After fueling, sniff for fumes and air out the boat thoroughly before starting up the engine.

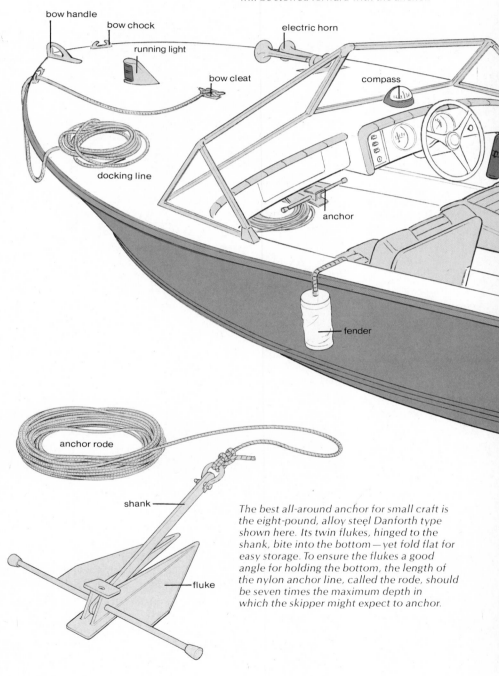

The runabout's vital equipment is carefully placed to be available when needed. The bow mooring line is run through a chock and cleated. Tool kit and life vests are kept under the seats, and buoyant cushions that double as extra lifesaving gear are quickly accessible. The first-aid kit, bilge pump and paddles are nestled against the starboard side of the hull; the fire extinguisher is within easy reach of the helmsman. Once underway, line and fenders will be stowed forward with the anchor.

bow handle

bow chock

running light

bow cleat

electric horn

compass

docking line

anchor

fender

anchor rode

shank

fluke

The best all-around anchor for small craft is the eight-pound, alloy steel Danforth type shown here. Its twin flukes, hinged to the shank, bite into the bottom—yet fold flat for easy storage. To ensure the flukes a good angle for holding the bottom, the length of the nylon anchor line, called the rode, should be seven times the maximum depth in which the skipper might expect to anchor.

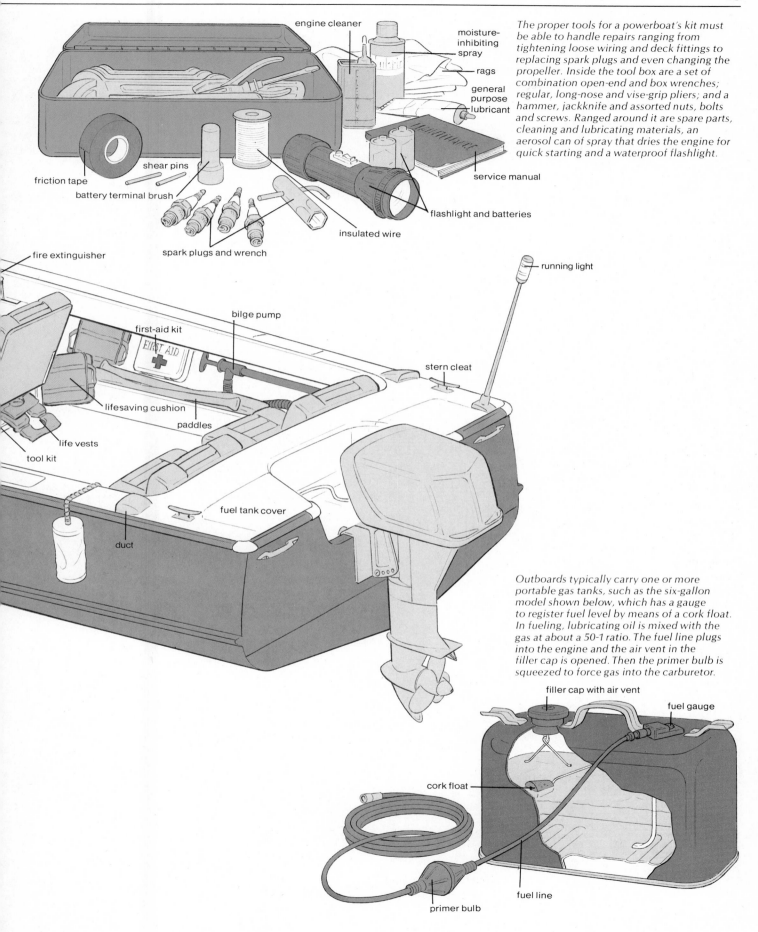

engine cleaner

moisture-inhibiting spray

rags

general purpose lubricant

The proper tools for a powerboat's kit must be able to handle repairs ranging from tightening loose wiring and deck fittings to replacing spark plugs and even changing the propeller. Inside the tool box are a set of combination open-end and box wrenches; regular, long-nose and vise-grip pliers; and a hammer, jackknife and assorted nuts, bolts and screws. Ranged around it are spare parts, cleaning and lubricating materials, an aerosol can of spray that dries the engine for quick starting and a waterproof flashlight.

service manual

friction tape

shear pins

battery terminal brush

spark plugs and wrench

insulated wire

flashlight and batteries

fire extinguisher

running light

bilge pump

first-aid kit

stern cleat

lifesaving cushion

paddles

life vests

tool kit

fuel tank cover

duct

Outboards typically carry one or more portable gas tanks, such as the six-gallon model shown below, which has a gauge to register fuel level by means of a cork float. In fueling, lubricating oil is mixed with the gas at about a 50-1 ratio. The fuel line plugs into the engine and the air vent in the filler cap is opened. Then the primer bulb is squeezed to force gas into the carburetor.

filler cap with air vent

fuel gauge

cork float

fuel line

primer bulb

Essential Safety Gear

Federal safety regulations divide boats into four categories according to length. Boats under 16 feet long are in class A; from 16 to less than 26 feet, class I; from 26 to less than 40 feet, class II; and from 40 to 65 feet, class III. The types and amounts of gear for each class are explained in the appendix *(page 168).*

However, certain general requirements apply in choosing safety gear for any size boat. All boats, for example, must carry Coast Guard-approved life preservers—officially called personal flotation devices, or PFDs. On powerboats, or sailboats with auxiliary engines, fire-fighting gear must also be approved by the Coast Guard, and it should be specifically designed to fight the commonest types of shipboard fires, those fueled by gas, oil or grease. Sound-making devices for use in fog and for right-of-way signals are required for all boats over 16 feet long.

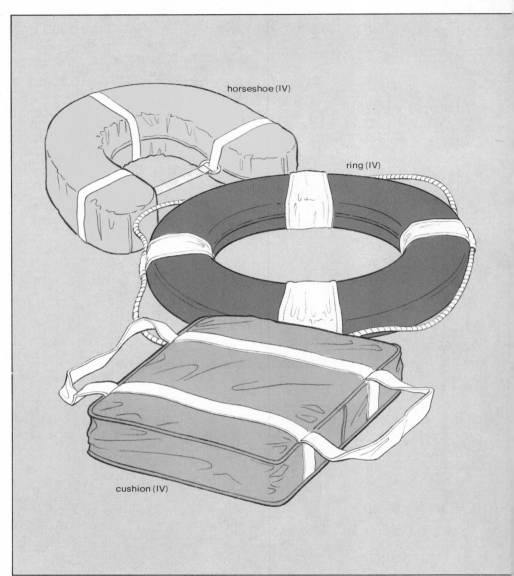

Both the hand-held Freon air horn and the electric-powered dual horns shown here satisfy the legal requirements for boats up to 65 feet in length. (Boats 26 feet and over must also have a bell.) The whistle, which should be audible for half a mile, meets the rules for boats less than 26 feet in length.

Personal flotation devices are classed as types I, II and III—the wearables shown at upper right—and type IV, which includes all the throwables above. Boats under 16 feet must carry one of the four types for each occupant, while bigger boats must carry a wearable type for each person, plus at least one throwable. Most recreational boatmen favor type III wearables, either vests or flotation jackets, because they are lighter and more comfortable. Bulkier types I or II, designed to turn an unconscious person face upward in the water, are recommended for commercial and cruising vessels. By law, type I must be orange. Throwable rings 20 inches or more in diameter are also orange—or white. Smaller ones, and all other flotation devices, should be brightly colored for maximum visibility.

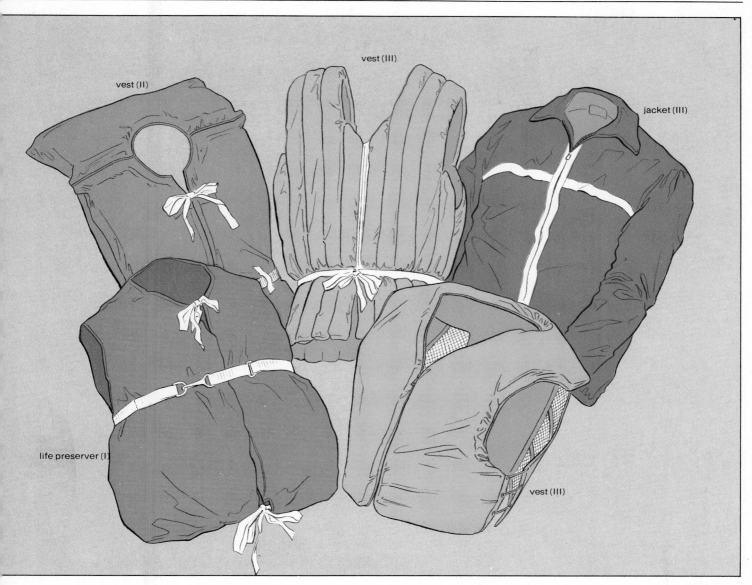

vest (III)

vest (II)

jacket (III)

life preserver (I)

vest (III)

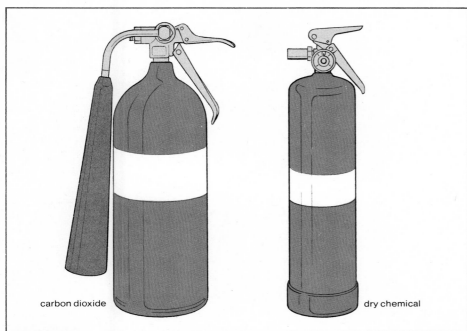

carbon dioxide

dry chemical

The two commonest kinds of portable marine fire extinguishers use either carbon dioxide or dry chemicals, both effective for oil or gas fires. Two other Coast Guard-approved types are foam—unpopular with boatmen because of the messy cleanup job afterward—and halon gas, which is a relatively new but effective flame-arresting element.

Starting the Engine

The sophisticated motorboats of today start almost as easily as does the family car. A modern inboard, with its automatic choke and self-priming fuel pump, is designed to kick over—and almost always does—whenever the driver hits the starter. After it idles briefly, the skipper can put the engine in gear and go.

The starting system for a standard outboard like the one at right is equally reliable, though the boatman usually has to operate the choke and priming systems by hand. To do so he first opens the air vent on the gas tank and squeezes the primer bulb to force fuel into the carburetor. Then, taking his place at the helm, he pulls out the choke knob to close down the choke, eases the throttle slightly forward and turns the ignition key. When the engine has idled a bit, he moves the choke back to its normal open position, and the boat is ready to leave.

This kind of dependability in starting prevails for virtually all modern boat motors, including the low-horsepower outboards employed on fishing boats and as sailboat auxiliaries. These are started by pulling a cord that spins the flywheel.

However, there are occasions when any engine may refuse to start. The skipper engages his starter, but the engine merely cranks over without catching—or doesn't crank at all. In such cases, the boatman usually can pinpoint the problem by going through the step-by-step procedures opposite. Some special tips for inboard starting appear below.

The majority of the time the engine will start running as the operator goes through this sequence of checks. And if the electric starting system on any outboard fails, he can always remove the engine cover, find the rope starter that is included for such emergencies, and crank by hand.

Tips for Inboards

The most frequent starting failures on inboards are due to wet ignition components. Often the skipper can solve the dampness problem simply by opening the engine compartment and airing it out; additionally he can dry off plugs, wiring and terminals with a cloth or by spraying them with a drying agent from an aerosol can.

Another problem can be that the engine is flooded. To clear it, he hits the starter and cranks the engine with the throttle wide open; after the engine starts, the throttle is pulled back to idle.

Remote controls for starting a modern outboard motor include a starter-ignition switch, a choke knob that pulls out for starting a cold engine, and a combination throttle-gearshift lever. The dashboard of this boat also has a fitting for a compass; a speedometer, and a tachometer to register rpm's, indicating how efficiently and economically the engine is performing. At far left, a row of buttons includes switches for the horns and for the bow and stern lights.

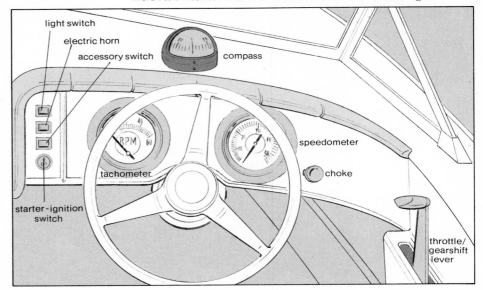

The electrical system, outlined in blue above, goes to work as the helmsman engages the dashboard starter switch, drawing current from the 12-volt battery and sending it to the starter solenoid. Essentially a relay, the solenoid links the battery and engine via heavy cables that can convey far greater amounts of power than the thin wires leading to and from the dashboard starter switch. When activated, the solenoid conducts power directly from the battery to the starter motor, which will turn the engine over and start it, provided that the gas tank has been fueled and the primer bulb squeezed.

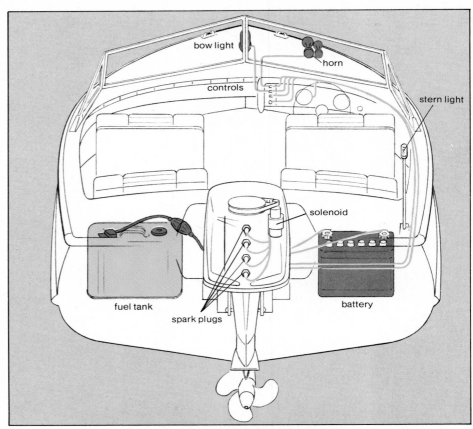

What to Do When the Engine Will Not Start

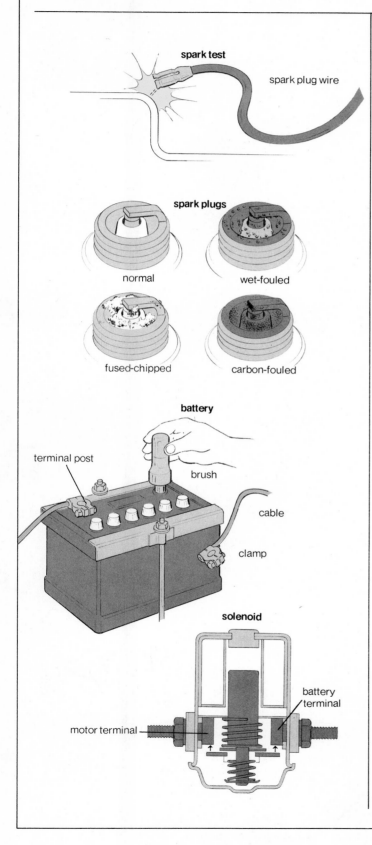

spark test

spark plug wire

spark plugs

normal

wet-fouled

fused-chipped

carbon-fouled

battery

terminal post

brush

cable

clamp

solenoid

motor terminal

battery terminal

Engine Cranks Over without Starting

1. Inspect the fuel supply, and be sure the tank's air vent is open; squeeze the primer bulb to guarantee that the carburetor is full. Set the choke properly: on a cold engine the knob is pulled out all the way to close the choke and enrich the fuel mixture. If the engine is warm, having been recently shut down, the choke knob should be pushed all the way forward, in its normal position.

2. After several futile starting attempts, engine cylinders may become so wet with fuel that combustion cannot occur. The engine is flooded. To clear it, open the choke, set the throttle full ahead and hit the starter. If the engine starts, leave the choke open and pull the throttle back to idle.

3. If the engine still does not start, test the spark and the spark plugs. First, remove the engine cover and make sure that the wires are firmly attached to the plugs and that they are dry. If they are wet, wipe them off or spray them with a drying agent available in an aerosol spray can. Then test the spark by removing one wire from a plug and holding the terminal about a quarter inch from the motor, as shown at left. Press the starter button; sparks should leap between the terminal and the metal. If there is no spark, the trouble is probably somewhere in the engine's wiring circuit, a problem that calls for expert help.

If there is a spark, remove all wires, unscrew the plugs and inspect the electrode points at their bases. A clean, functioning plug is illustrated at left along with three troublemakers. Points fouled with oil or carbon can be sanded or brushed clean; plugs with fused or damaged points should be replaced. Before putting the plugs back in, clear excess fuel from the engine by cranking it; this will prevent flooding. While cranking, ground the spark plug to the metal of the engine. Otherwise, voltage generated by the ignition system could build up and cause severe damage. With plugs and wires back in place, try the starter again. If the engine does not kick over now, it is time to call a mechanic.

Starter Is Engaged and Nothing Happens

1. Make sure the battery cables are firmly clamped at the battery and engine terminals. Then try the light switch—if the lights are dim or out, the battery may be weak or dead. If the lights are bright, leave them on and hit the starter again. If the lights dim now, the problem may be a weak battery or bad terminal connections. Remove the cables and clean the terminals and clamps with sandpaper, steel wool or a steel brush such as the one shown at left; then firmly reclamp the cables to the battery.

2. If the battery appears adequately charged and the terminal connections are clean and tight, the problem could be in the starter solenoid, shown at lower left. When the dashboard starter switch is engaged, the central shaft of the solenoid should lift, putting the disc on the lower part of the shaft in contact with the internal terminals for the battery and engine. When this happens there should be an audible click from the solenoid. If there is no click, the solenoid is not working either because it is defective or because of bad wiring between it and the dashboard switch.

3. A defective solenoid must be replaced, but before calling a mechanic, give the wiring system a quick final check. With the ignition off, begin at the dashboard starter switch and trace back toward the engine, looking for loose, frayed or damaged wires that may have broken the flow of current.

Preparing a Sailboat

The sailboat skipper, like the powerboat-man, should preface every trip by checking his gear. His craft carries many of the same items needed on an outboard, such as a paddle, an anchor and rode, extra line for docking or being towed, life preservers and a first-aid kit. The sailor's repair kit, however, should include line, tape and tools for mending sails and rigging. For rough-weather sailing, he should have a bucket to backstop his bilge pump.

On the 19-foot sloop at right, all portable gear has been stowed. The skipper next inspects the shrouds and headstay to make sure that they are properly taut and securely fastened.

If he were sailing this boat for the first time, he would also check the location of fairleads and cleats for the sheets and halyards. Finally, he attaches the rudder as shown at far right; he is then ready to put on his sails (pages 26-27).

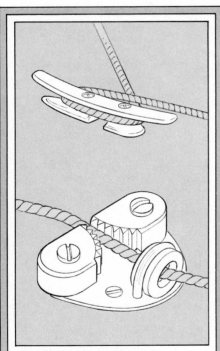

Quick-action Cleats

Many small sailboats carry specialized cleats like the ones above for securing main and jib sheets, which may have to be tied down or released in a hurry. With the jam cleat, one turn and a tug will wedge a line under the cleat's long shoulder. The cam cleat grips a line between two swiveling, serrated cams; simply jerking the line up releases it. If the serration wears down after long use, the cams will not get a grip on the line, and they should be renewed. A fairlead guides the line through the cams.

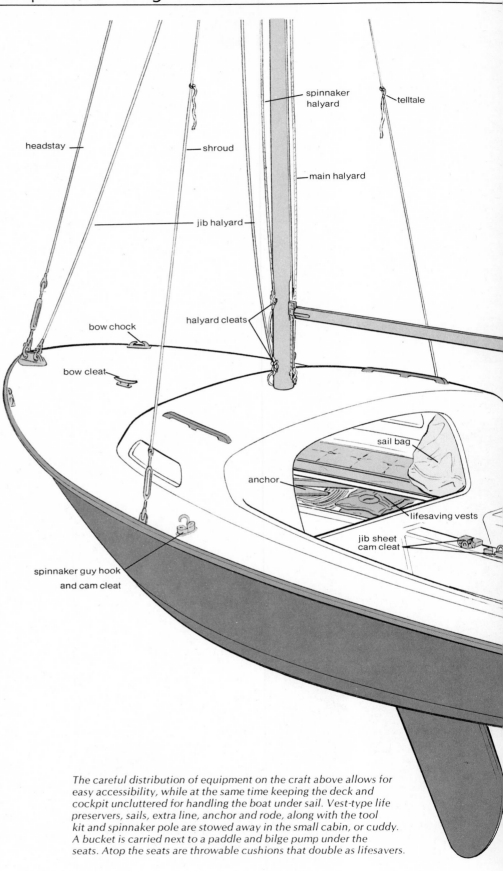

The careful distribution of equipment on the craft above allows for easy accessibility, while at the same time keeping the deck and cockpit uncluttered for handling the boat under sail. Vest-type life preservers, sails, extra line, anchor and rode, along with the tool kit and spinnaker pole are stowed away in the small cabin, or cuddy. A bucket is carried next to a paddle and bilge pump under the seats. Atop the seats are throwable cushions that double as lifesavers.

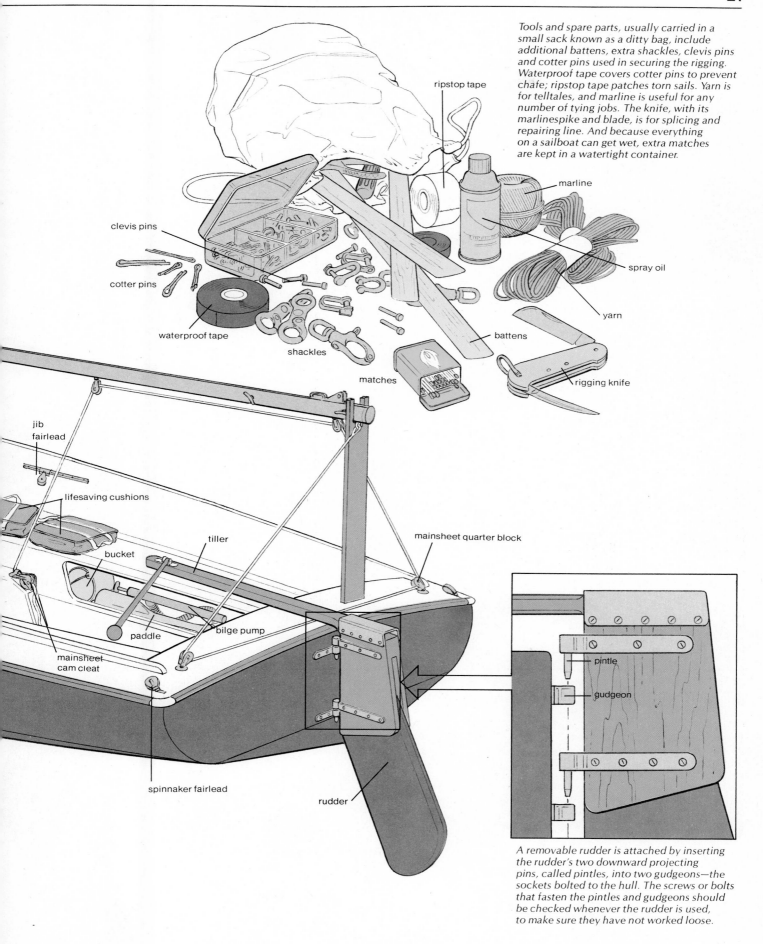

Tools and spare parts, usually carried in a small sack known as a ditty bag, include additional battens, extra shackles, clevis pins and cotter pins used in securing the rigging. Waterproof tape covers cotter pins to prevent chafe; ripstop tape patches torn sails. Yarn is for telltales, and marline is useful for any number of tying jobs. The knife, with its marlinespike and blade, is for splicing and repairing line. And because everything on a sailboat can get wet, extra matches are kept in a watertight container.

ripstop tape

clevis pins

cotter pins

waterproof tape

shackles

matches

battens

marline

spray oil

yarn

rigging knife

jib fairlead

lifesaving cushions

tiller

bucket

paddle

bilge pump

mainsheet cam cleat

mainsheet quarter block

spinnaker fairlead

rudder

pintle

gudgeon

A removable rudder is attached by inserting the rudder's two downward projecting pins, called pintles, into two gudgeons—the sockets bolted to the hull. The screws or bolts that fasten the pintles and gudgeons should be checked whenever the rudder is used, to make sure they have not worked loose.

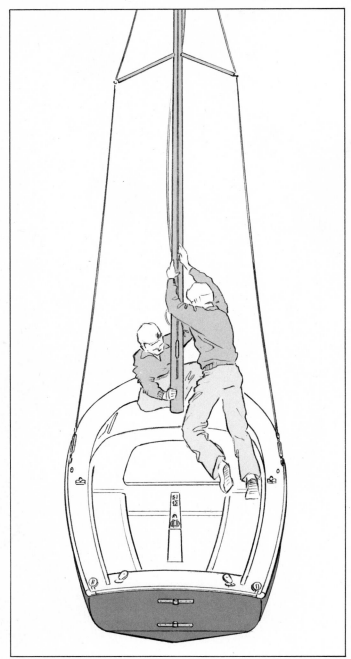

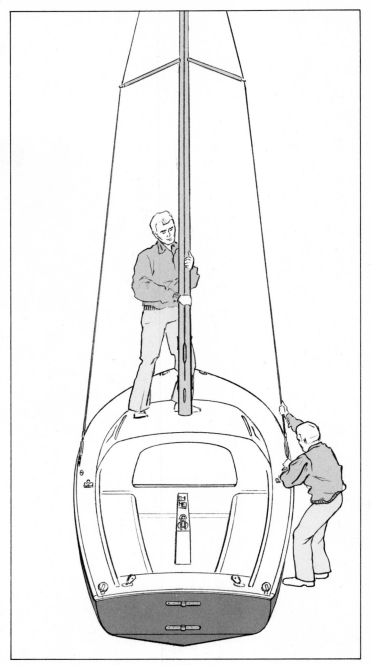

Putting up the mast, one man guides its heel
onto the mast step while the other walks
it upright. To help steady the mast while it is
raised, the shrouds have been attached
to their fittings on either side of the hull. The
halyards have been run through their
blocks and cleated; the headstay is loosely
wound around the mast to keep it out of
the way. Once the mast is in place, its heel
should fit with no more than half an inch
of sideways movement. If too loose, the mast
should be temporarily unstepped so that
wedges can be taped inside the mast step.

While one sailor holds the mast steady, the
other, having first attached the headstay,
takes up the slack in the shrouds by adjusting
the turnbuckles. (If the boat carried a
backstay, that would be fastened next.) With
the shrouds and headstay taut, the skipper
makes sure the mast is straight by sighting up
along it and by studying it as he walks
around the boat. After making corrections in
the rigging, he slips cotter pins into each
turnbuckle to prevent further turning. Then
he should wrap tape over the points of
the pins to prevent sails from being ripped.

Stepping the Mast

The masts on most sailboats are usually put up once a year, at the beginning of the season. On many trailer-borne craft, however, the mast must be erected at each launching. The operation is called stepping because the heel of the mast fits into a socket known as a mast step.

Before putting the mast into position *(left)*, the skipper should check the fittings that secure the rigging and the boom to the mast, as shown at right. The simplest fitting is an eye on the front of the mast for attaching the spinnaker pole. Standard fittings for shrouds and stay, shown at right, are for a boat with a fractional rig, where the headstay reaches only part way up the mast. On a masthead rig the shrouds and headstay would attach at the masthead fitting. This boat has no backstay, since its shrouds are angled slightly aft; if there were a backstay, it too would attach to the masthead.

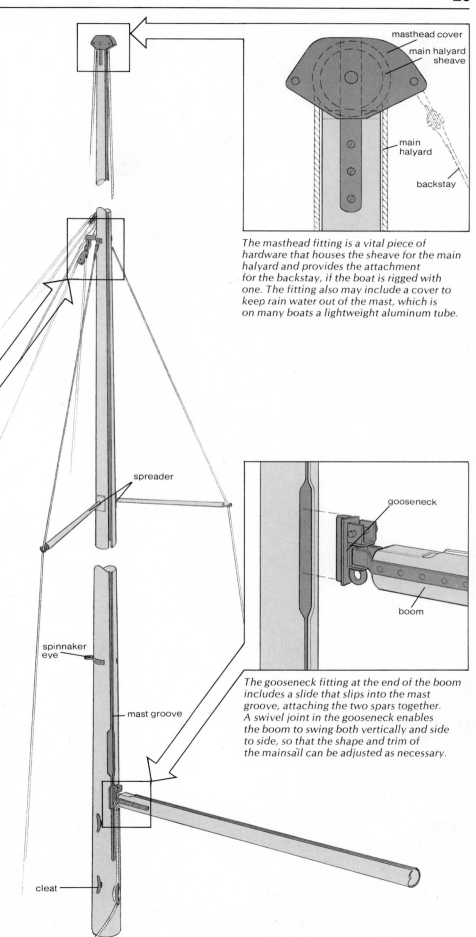

The masthead fitting is a vital piece of hardware that houses the sheave for the main halyard and provides the attachment for the backstay, if the boat is rigged with one. The fitting also may include a cover to keep rain water out of the mast, which is on many boats a lightweight aluminum tube.

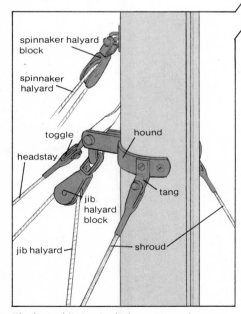

The hound fitting includes two metal straps bolted to the mast to grip the upper ends of the shrouds, jib halyard and headstay. The jib halyard block fastens with a shackle, the headstay with a fitting called a toggle, the shrouds to metal strips called tangs. Above the hound is a spinnaker halyard block.

The gooseneck fitting at the end of the boom includes a slide that slips into the mast groove, attaching the two spars together. A swivel joint in the gooseneck enables the boom to swing both vertically and side to side, so that the shape and trim of the mainsail can be adjusted as necessary.

Checking Out the Sails

Each time sails are pulled from their bags, they ought to be given a quick inspection for tears, wear and fraying. Even minor flaws, unless fixed by a sailmaker or temporarily patched up with tape, can turn into serious, expensive damage if the cloth rends in strong wind.

The most vulnerable areas are the edges and corners, which are subject to the greatest tension. In sailors' parlance, the sail's leading edge is its luff, the trailing edge its leech and the bottom its foot. The term for the top corner is the head, while the lower forward corner is called the tack and the trailing one the clew. Lines known as boltropes take the strain on the luff and foot of the mainsail, while a luff wire or sometimes a rope fortifies the jib; the stitching on both should be examined for loose ends. Extra layers of fabric, or patches, reinforce the corners, which also have metal eyes, called cringles, used to attach the sail to the boat, the spars or running rigging. The cringles come under great stress and should be checked to ensure that they have not worked loose.

The Search for a Better Sail

Since the days of the first sailing craft, mariners have sought better fabrics to hoist on their masts. Ancient Egyptians tried leather; Columbus used linen; 19th Century clipper ships flew light, sturdy cotton canvas. But all these natural materials mildewed when wet, lost their shape with use and rotted with old age. Not until the development of synthetic fibers in the 1940s were these problems overcome. Here are the synthetics that have come closest to ending the ancient search for an ideal sailcloth:

Nylon is strong and resistant to rot and mildew. Because its filament is inherently stretchy, nylon is not ideal for working sails that must hold their shape; but it is just right for spinnakers and other full-bellied, lightweight sails.
Dacron (called Terylene in some parts of the world) was developed in the early 1950s. It is light, strong and impervious to rot, and has little stretch. Thus Dacron sails can be precisely cut and will hold their shape well. Today most working sails are made of Dacron.
Kevlar is a synthetic that has been used on some successful racing boats. Its fibers have the tensile strength of steel and virtually no stretch. But its brittleness and a tendency to deteriorate in sunlight must be overcome before Kevlar becomes everyman's sailcloth.

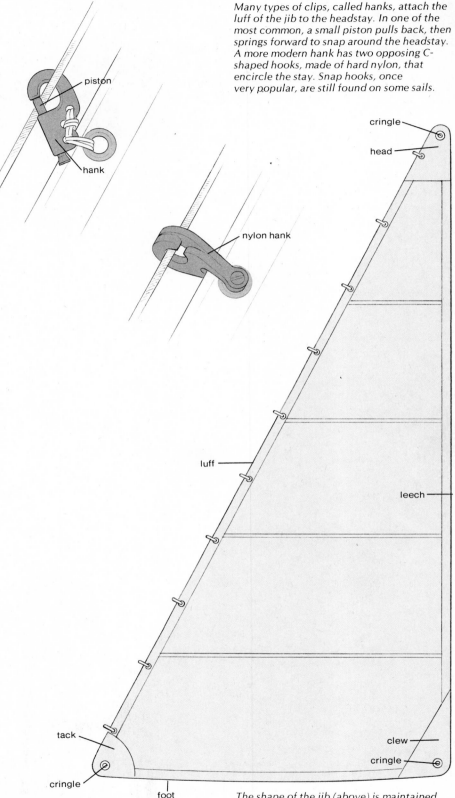

Many types of clips, called hanks, attach the luff of the jib to the headstay. In one of the most common, a small piston pulls back, then springs forward to snap around the headstay. A more modern hank has two opposing C-shaped hooks, made of hard nylon, that encircle the stay. Snap hooks, once very popular, are still found on some sails.

The shape of the jib (above) is maintained underway by the pull of its halyard, which draws the luff taut along the headstay, and by tension on the jibsheet attached to the clew. On a small jib like this, all the panels of sailcloth are horizontal. Larger jibs are miter-cut: a diagonal seam runs from clew to luff. The panels above it are horizontal and those below it are vertical, a design that adds strength where the strain is greatest.

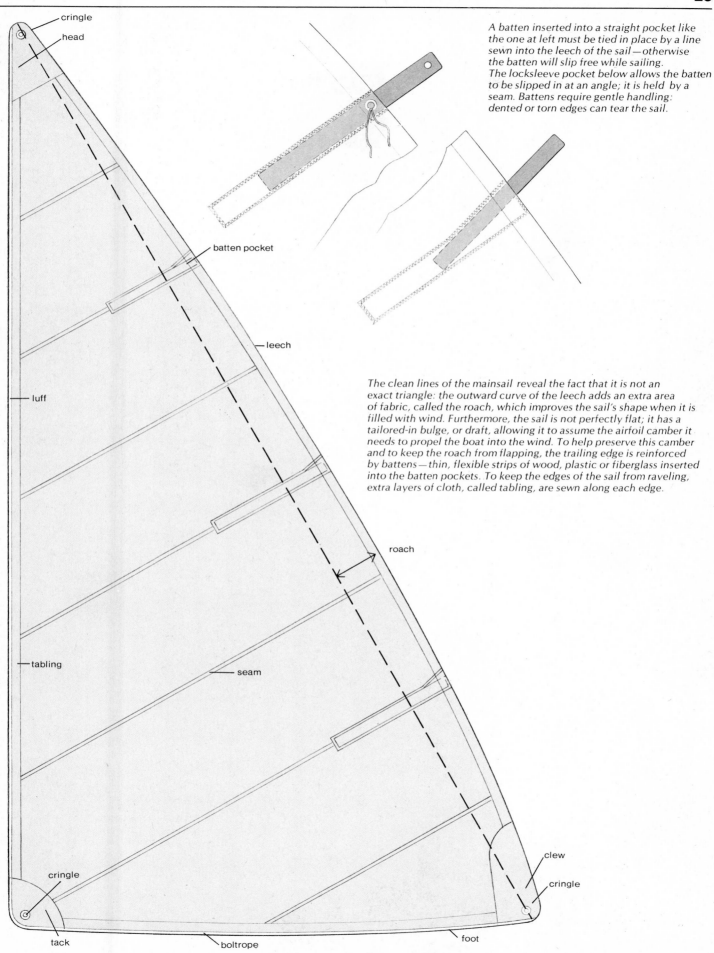

A batten inserted into a straight pocket like the one at left must be tied in place by a line sewn into the leech of the sail—otherwise the batten will slip free while sailing. The locksleeve pocket below allows the batten to be slipped in at an angle; it is held by a seam. Battens require gentle handling: dented or torn edges can tear the sail.

The clean lines of the mainsail reveal the fact that it is not an exact triangle: the outward curve of the leech adds an extra area of fabric, called the roach, which improves the sail's shape when it is filled with wind. Furthermore, the sail is not perfectly flat; it has a tailored-in bulge, or draft, allowing it to assume the airfoil camber it needs to propel the boat into the wind. To help preserve this camber and to keep the roach from flapping, the trailing edge is reinforced by battens—thin, flexible strips of wood, plastic or fiberglass inserted into the batten pockets. To keep the edges of the sail from raveling, extra layers of cloth, called tabling, are sewn along each edge.

cringle

head

batten pocket

leech

luff

roach

tabling

seam

clew

cringle

cringle

tack

boltrope

foot

Bending On Sails

The sails for all boats are put on in much the same way, though details of equipment and technique vary widely. First the jib is attached to the headstay; then the mainsail is strung out along the boom and mast. On some boats the spars have grooves, into which boltropes along the sail's luff and foot are threaded. On other craft metal slides are secured at intervals along the boltrope, and these are slipped onto tracks or into grooves on the spars.

Before putting up the sails on a small boat it is a good idea to lower the centerboard. This will help hold the craft stable as the skipper moves around in it. Also, the skipper should check sails and lines to be sure they have no twists or tangles.

To tighten the mainsail once it is up, many boats have an outhaul, shown at bottom right, at the end of the boom and a downhaul at the gooseneck that lowers the boom and draws taut the luff.

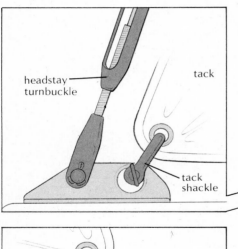

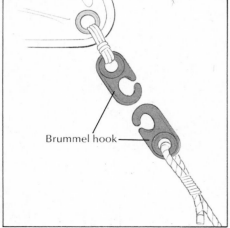

The jib tack is attached to the stemhead fitting (top) with a shackle. Then the luff hanks are put on the headstay, working up from the tack. The jib sheets attach, in this case with Brummel hooks, one on the sail's clew and one on the paired sheets. The hooks join when their narrow openings slide together at right angles to each other.

Having bent on the jib and attached its halyard with a shackle to the head (above, left), the sailor performs the two-step process of putting on the main. First, the foot of the sail is fitted to the boom by inserting the boltrope into the groove, starting with the clew, and sliding it out to the end of the boom, where it is secured to the outhaul. Then the tack is attached with a pin to the gooseneck. Second, the main halyard is shackled to the head and the top of the luff boltrope is slipped into the mast groove, as shown in the detailed drawing above.

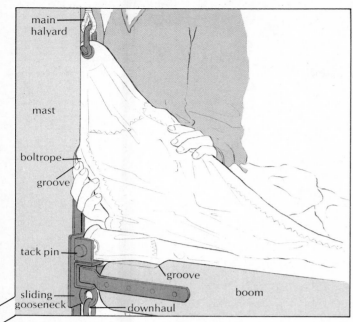

main
halyard

mast

boltrope

groove

tack pin

sliding
gooseneck

downhaul

groove

boom

The boltrope in the luff of the mainsail enters
head first into the mast groove near the
gooseneck fitting (above). To prevent the
rope from jamming as it travels up the mast,
the sailor must carefully feed it into
the groove by hand while he hoists the sail.

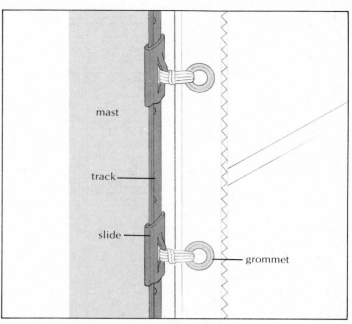

mast

track

slide

grommet

Instead of fitting into a groove, the mainsail
is often bent on by metal slides that run on a
track. A mast track usually has a swiveling
section, or gate, above the boom. With the
gate open the slides are slipped on one by
one; the gate is then closed before hoisting.

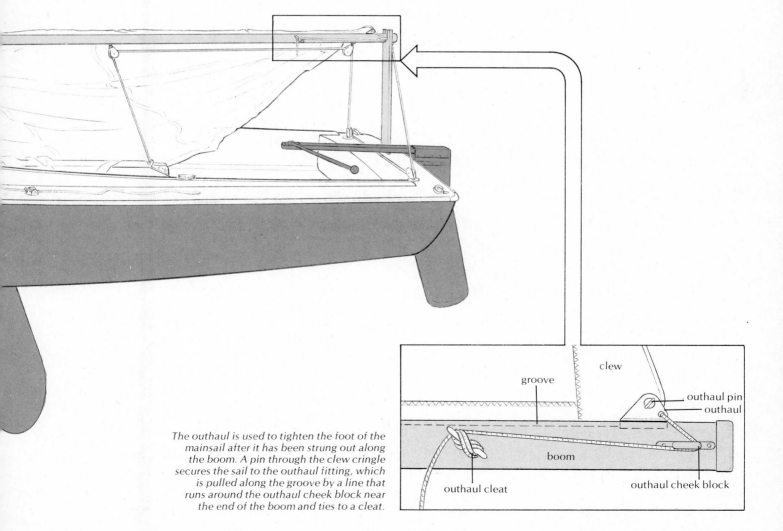

clew

groove

outhaul pin

outhaul

boom

outhaul cleat

outhaul cheek block

The outhaul is used to tighten the foot of the
mainsail after it has been strung out along
the boom. A pin through the clew cringle
secures the sail to the outhaul fitting, which
is pulled along the groove by a line that
runs around the outhaul cheek block near
the end of the boom and ties to a cleat.

If the wind is blowing across a dock or slip (below), the skipper must move his boat so the bow is pointing into the wind before he hauls up the sails. Otherwise the sails will blow sideways onto the dock, or drive the boat into it. To position his craft correctly, the sailor first releases the docking lines. Taking the bow line off the bollard, or mooring post, and fending off the hull as he goes, he walks the boat out to the end of the slip, angling the stern around so that the bow heads into the wind. After securing the bow line again—and putting out fenders to keep the boat from rubbing against the dock—he is ready to hoist the sails with the bow lying properly head to the wind.

Hoisting the Sails

When hoisting sails, the first step is to determine which way the breeze is blowing. Sails should always be hauled up with the boat headed into the wind. Otherwise the wind may catch the sails from the side or rear, filling them prematurely and making them impossible to hoist. At a mooring, wind direction is no problem, since a boat responds like a weather vane and heads naturally into the wind.

At a dock or slip, however, where the boat is not free to swing, the skipper should always check his telltales *(below)* to establish the wind direction. If the wind is coming from the side, or astern, he will have to move his boat so that it lies with the bow pointing into the wind, as shown at left, below.

With his boat in position, the skipper makes sure his sheets are not cleated, so that the sail will luff freely as it rises. He hoists the mainsail first, because wind pressure against even the loosely luffing canvas will help keep the bow pointed in the right direction. He pulls up the halyard in a smooth, easy motion until the head of the sail reaches the mast top, then secures the halyard to its cleat. Next, he hoists the jib and secures its halyard. The ends of the halyards should be neatly coiled and hung over a cleat—they must run free if the sails are lowered in a hurry. With the canvas aloft, the skipper makes a few final adjustments *(right)* and is ready to cast off and go sailing.

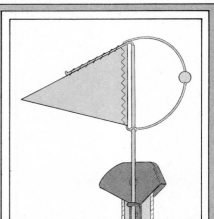

A Telltale for the Wind

To learn the direction of the wind, most sailors use a mast-top wind indicator or telltale such as this marine weather vane, called a masthead fly. Simpler telltales—bits of ribbon or wool yarn tied to a shroud or stay—may also serve. On some large boats, electronic sensing devices atop the mast give both the wind's direction and its speed.

His sails hoisted, the skipper may have to adjust tension along
the luff and foot of the mainsail and on the luff of the jib, to give the
sails a proper aerodynamic shape when full of wind. In general, if the
main halyard and outhaul are pulled too tight, pronounced wrinkles
will appear parallel with the luff and foot as shown in the drawing
directly below. If the luff and foot are too loose, as in the lower
diagram, the symptom will be puckers or scallops. For any particular
day, the right tension depends on the wind strength: in light air,
tension should be light; in stronger wind, the sails are set up tighter.

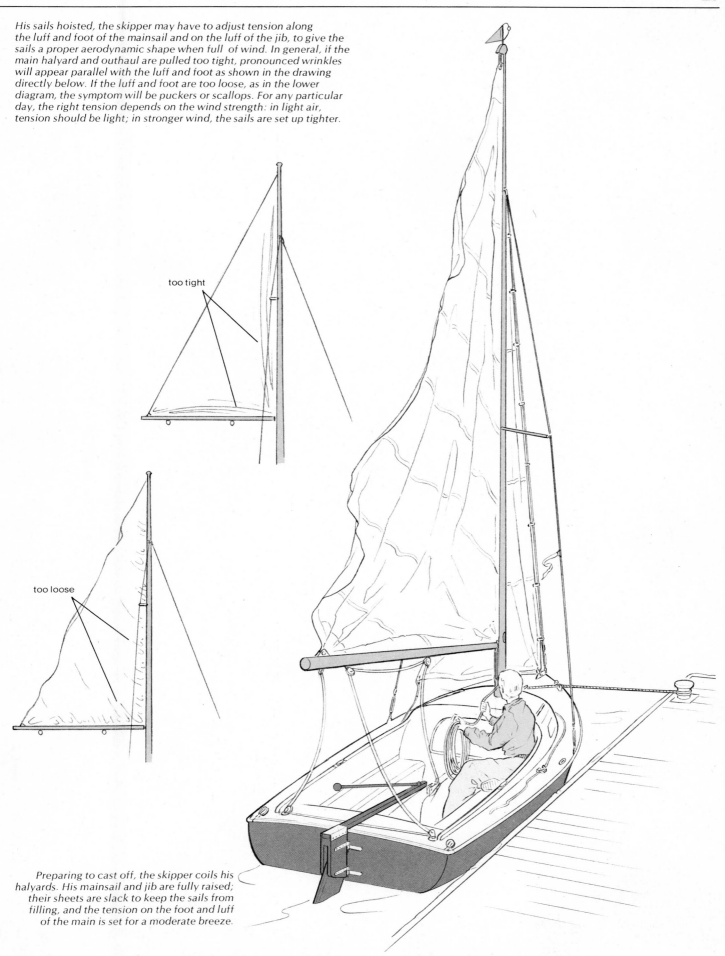

too tight

too loose

Preparing to cast off, the skipper coils his
halyards. His mainsail and jib are fully raised;
their sheets are slack to keep the sails from
filling, and the tension on the foot and luff
of the main is set for a moderate breeze.

ROWING: A CLASSIC WAY TO GET STARTED

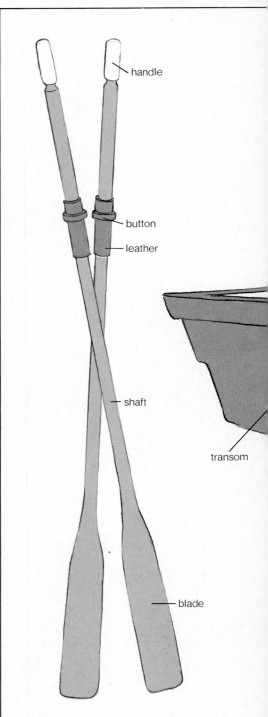

For many a skipper whose boat lies at a mooring or at anchor, a necessary prelude to getting underway is to ferry himself, his crew and supplies out to his vessel in a rowboat, or dinghy. He thus finds himself traveling aboard the most basic of waterborne craft, and employing the most fundamental of boathandling skills.

Indeed, rowing is the first experience many yachtsmen have with boats. Furthermore, it is a skill every sailor should acquire. For, while some dinghies carry a mounting block on the transom to accommodate a small outboard motor, many others do not. And in any case, small outboards are likely to balk, leaving a pair of oars the only alternative.

A practical dinghy for cruising boats is a skiff such as the 12-footer at right, or a smaller version of the same design. It has a relatively flat bottom for stability, a pointed bow for cutting through choppy water and plenty of room for passengers and gear. The smaller pram, which has a squared-off bow for compactness, is preferred for vessels of 30 feet or less.

The majority of today's prams and skiffs are made of fiberglass, which is strong, durable and simple to maintain. Those made of aluminum are lighter and generally cheaper. Wooden dinghies cost more, and must be painted or varnished annually, but they have a beauty that many yachtsmen admire.

A dinghy's oars vary in size according to the dimensions of the boat and the rower's preference: strong, large-limbed oarsmen usually like long oars. In general, though, a 10-foot skiff requires oars five and a half to six and a half feet long. Oarlocks, which supply the essential connection between oars and boat, are usually made of metal—either galvanized iron or steel, or bronze, though sometimes they are nothing more than two pairs of thick wooden pegs, called thole pins, that are fitted into the gunwale.

The best oars are made of durable ash or springy spruce. The collar around the shaft, known as the leather, has a ridge, called a button, which keeps the oar from sliding out through the oarlock. Though the shafts and blades of oars are usually painted as protection against rot and weathering, the handles should be left bare: clean wood is easier to grip and causes fewer blisters.

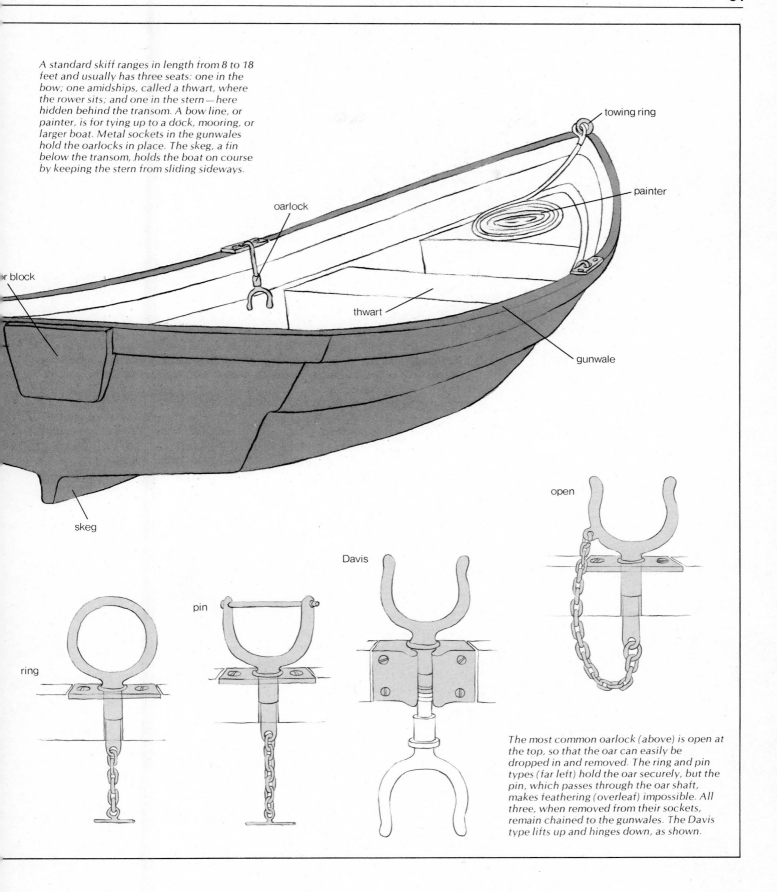

A standard skiff ranges in length from 8 to 18 feet and usually has three seats: one in the bow; one amidships, called a thwart, where the rower sits; and one in the stern—here hidden behind the transom. A bow line, or painter, is for tying up to a dock, mooring, or larger boat. Metal sockets in the gunwales hold the oarlocks in place. The skeg, a fin below the transom, holds the boat on course by keeping the stern from sliding sideways.

towing ring

painter

oarlock

thwart

gunwale

or block

skeg

open

Davis

pin

ring

The most common oarlock (above) is open at the top, so that the oar can easily be dropped in and removed. The ring and pin types (far left) hold the oar securely, but the pin, which passes through the oar shaft, makes teathering (overleaf) impossible. All three, when removed from their sockets, remain chained to the gunwales. The Davis type lifts up and hinges down, as shown.

The Basic Stroke

Before an oarsman takes his first stroke, he must make one fundamental but sometimes tricky step—into the boat. Unless he steps carefully amidships, keeping his knees bent and his weight low, he may lurch overboard or capsize the boat. He can steady himself by putting a hand on each gunwale, but he should be ready to grab the dock with one hand if the boat starts to float away.

Then, seated on the thwart, facing aft, he secures the outside oarlock in its socket and puts the outside oar in the oarlock. Then he pushes away from the dock, using either his hand or the other oar.

Once away from the dock, the oarsman positions the second oarlock and oar, and gets ready to row ahead, using the basic sweep stroke detailed on these pages. Since he is facing the stern, he will have to glance over his shoulder from time to time to see where he is going. Or he can line up the middle of the transom with a fixed point ashore, and use one of the course-correcting techniques described on the following pages to keep himself going in the right direction.

Beginning the sweep stroke, the oarsman leans forward in the catch position. Holding the oar blades vertical, he drops them cleanly into the water. His feet are securely braced against a stretcher—a cross-piece installed in some rowboats to give the oarsman a foothold. If there is no stretcher, he braces against the stern seat or a rib.

The Deft Art of Feathering

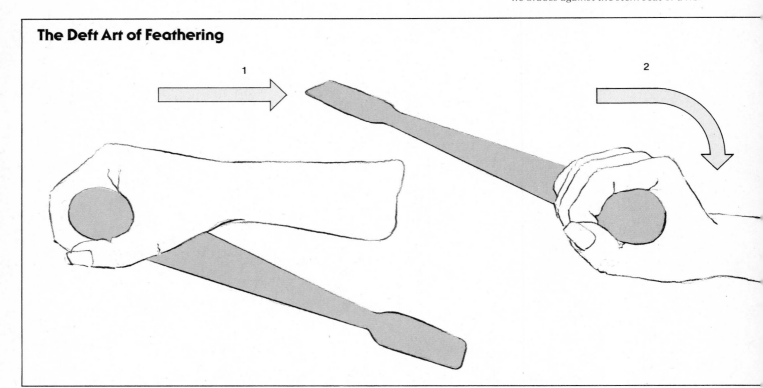

Making the stroke, the rower gets the oars moving by straightening back from the catch position, at the same time driving with his legs. At first he keeps his arms straight, but as the boat gathers momentum, he pulls them in, while holding his back erect. Near the end of the stroke, he eases up to allow the boat to glide forward.

At the finish the oarsman lifts the blades out of the water for the so-called feathered recovery (below). In lifting, he neither pushes down too hard on the handles, which would carry the blades too high above the water; nor too lightly, which might allow a blade to be caught by the water and bury itself — a mishap known as catching a crab.

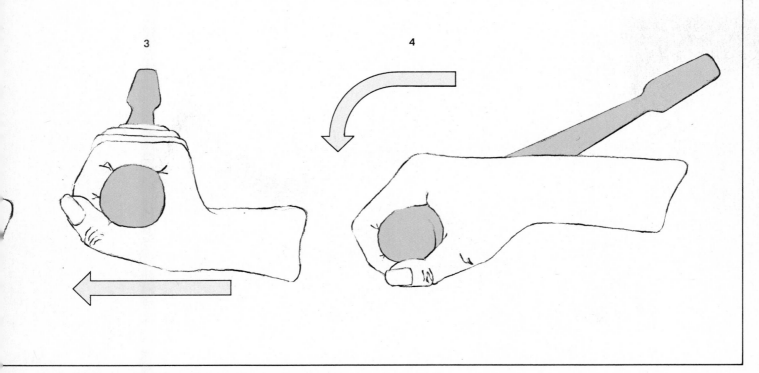

Feathering is a muscle-saving refinement that good oarsmen use during the recovery to keep the oars skimming low over the water so that the wind or waves will not catch the blades. During the actual stroke, the oarsman keeps each wrist horizontal (1). But as he removes the blade at the finish (2), he drops his wrist to turn — or feather — the blade almost parallel to the water. During the recovery, he keeps his wrist bent (3). Then, straightening his wrist (4), he rotates the blade 90°, and prepares to drop it into the water for the next pull.

The Oarsman's Brakes

When an oarsman wants to slow down to stop or to travel backward, he does just what a motorboater does: he goes into reverse. In the oarsman's case, he employs a modified reversal of the sweep stroke shown on the preceding pages.

To slow the boat he simply holds the oars still in mid-stroke with blades vertical. A firm push on the handles will then bring him to a dead stop. A continuing sequence of pushes changes the stopping action into a full reverse stroke, called backwatering, shown at right.

In the catch position of the backwater stroke the oarsman sits upright, elbows bent and wrists close to his body, with the oar blades held perpendicular to the water. After dropping the blades in, he pushes away on the oar handles in a short, choppy stroke that best uses weight and muscle to overcome water resistance against the flat transom.

The Wide Turn

The simplest method for turning is to stop rowing with one oar and continue pulling with the other, as in the photograph at the immediate right. The result is a wide turn *(below)*, which is used most often to correct course or to approach a dock.

When making turns, the oarsman must remember that since he is facing backward, his directional references are reversed: port is to his right, and starboard to his left. Thus a pull with his left hand, which controls the starboard oar, will turn the boat to port, and vice versa.

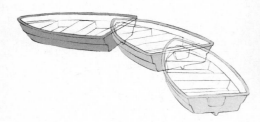

Keeping his body firmly centered in the boat, the oarsman turns to the left by pulling with his starboard oar. He holds the port oar balanced in the oarlock, its feathered blade well clear of the water. Trailing the idle oar in the water would turn it into a brake and result in a more acute turn, but would also slow the boat's forward momentum.

When his oars are almost at right angles to the gunwales, and before his arms are fully extended, the oarsman begins to lift the blades out of the water, ready to return to the catch position. He must not push down too hard before the end of the stroke or the oars will come out of the water too soon, wasting effort and cutting momentum.

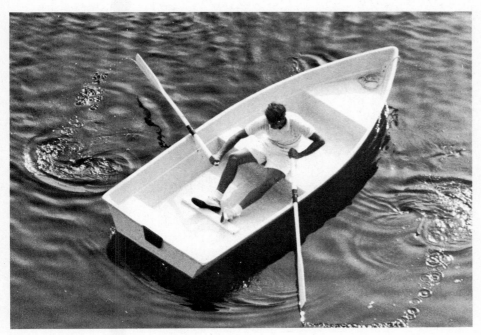

His feet braced against the stretcher, the oarsman executes a clockwise pivot by pulling with his right-hand, or port, oar and pushing with his left-hand, or starboard, oar. The whorls on either side of the boat show where the oars left the water on the previous stroke. Reversing this push-pull motion would rotate the boat counterclockwise.

The Pivot Turn

When an oarsman needs to swivel his boat around in a confined space, such as a crowded river or marina, he uses a pivot turn, in which he pulls on one oar in a normal sweep stroke, while backwatering with the other. This maneuver spins the boat around on its center point, as illustrated in the diagram below.

As in all turns, the oarsman will keep better control if he uses a succession of short, quick arm-strokes, rather than trying to muscle the boat around with a single, backstraining heave.

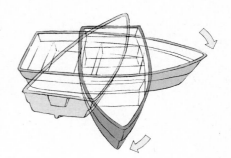

Final Swing to the Dock

Timing is the most important factor in bringing a rowboat in to a landing. The oarsman must gauge the effect of wind and current on the speed of his boat; whenever possible, he should approach against the wind or current to keep from being swept in too quickly. He must turn at just the right moment to bring himself parallel to the dock, as in the pictures at right. If he approaches too slowly, or turns prematurely, he will not reach the dock. If he comes in too energetically, or turns too late, he may hit head-on. And he must be ready to ship his oars and oarlocks to avoid jamming them under the dock—or if coming up to a larger vessel, to keep them from gouging its topsides.

Approaching the dock, the oarsman has given a pull with his left-hand oar, turning the boat's bow to port and causing the boat to start coming around parallel to the dock. In order to tighten the turn and increase his control over the boat, the oarsman is about to drop his outside oar into the water with the blade vertical to act as a pivot point.

Sculling: A Useful Skill

To slip through places too narrow for rowing—or to surmount that embarrassing moment when an oar drops overboard—every sailor should master the useful art of sculling. In sculling, a single oar, held by a notch or oarlock in the transom, is moved back and forth in an underhand-overhand motion that propels the boat in somewhat the same way a fish's tail propels its body. Sculling can be performed sitting, kneeling or standing. The key to the stroke is the angle of the blade, determined by the angle of the wrist. If the blade is too vertical the stern will swing wildly back and forth; if too flat, the oar will slice ineffectually through the water and the boat will not move at all.

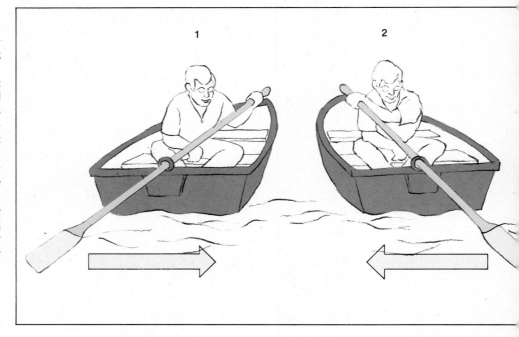

By backwatering with his outside oar, the oarsman slows the boat's forward speed, at the same time pivoting the stern toward the dock and giving the boat some sideways momentum. To keep his inside oar from getting caught between the dock and the side of the boat, he pulls the oar inboard, resting the shaft temporarily in the oarlock.

Just before the boat touches the dock, the oarsman takes his inside oar from the oarlock and drops it into the boat, parallel to the gunwale. Quickly, he removes the oarlock from its socket, then ships the outside oar and oarlock. Finally, he will grab the dock to keep from drifting away, picking up the boat's painter as he prepares to step ashore.

The sculling stroke begins with the oar held in one hand, as in step 1. The sculler moves the handle to his right, dropping his wrist as he goes to keep the blade at the same angle. At the end of the arc, he lifts his wrist to angle the blade in the opposite direction (2) so that the same side of the blade pushes against the water. He now pulls the handle back (3) and drops his wrist to return the blade to its original angle (4). Repeating the stroke (5), he swings through a rhythmic sequence that moves the boat in the zigzag course shown at left.

ROWING IN ITS HEYDAY

Before the gasoline engine went to sea, when the boatman's only means of loco- motion was by wind or oar, the rowboat was the workhorse of the water. Salmon fishermen in Alaska and lobstermen in Maine rowed themselves to work. Brave men in stout lifeboats fought heavy surf and gale winds to rescue shipwrecked mariners. Fleets of small pulling boats swarmed like waterbugs around the na- tion's busy seaports, ferrying passengers and produce from ship to shore.

Special rowboats evolved for specific tasks: deep-bellied dories for offshore fishing; flat-bottomed skiffs for skimming along lakes and rivers; sturdy 30-foot whaleboats for harpooning great blue and sperm whales from the Arctic Ocean to the Tasman Sea.

People also rowed just for sport. Rival bargemen, who had been racing out to meet ships entering New York Harbor since the 17th Century, eventually began betting a few dollars on who would get there first. There were lifeboat races, whaleboat races and dory races, attract- ing crowds of watchers on shore. In the mid-1830s amateur rowing clubs began sprouting up, and special long, narrow racing craft called shells, like the ones at right, were designed solely for speed.

Crew racing became one of the biggest sports in America in the second half of the century. Hundreds of spectators watched Harvard sweep ahead of Yale in the coun- try's first intercollegiate crew race in 1852, 22 years before anyone even consid- ered going to a football game. Thousands of dollars changed hands on the outcome of professional regattas, and champion oarsmen became Saturday's heroes.

Eventually the pros dropped out of row- ing, and working rowboats gave way to gasoline-powered vessels. Today people row simply for pleasure—the duck hunter in his punt, the crewman in his shell and the yachtsman in his dinghy.

Displaying a splendid array of racing shells, members of a New York City boat club of the last century gather outside their Harlem River boathouse. In the six- and eight-oared shells at left, each man pulls a single oar, as a coxswain rides astern to steer and to call the stroke. The crews of one-man sculls ply both oars and set their own rhythm.

Lifeboats, each pulled by eight oarsmen and steered by a coxswain, sprint past Pier A near the southern tip of New York City during a Labor Day regatta in the late 1920s. The boats were competing in the annual running of the International Lifeboat Race, in which the world's major steamship companies took part. Any ship in port on the day of the race could enter one of its lifeboats, manned by members of the ship's crew. Norwegian and Italian boats usually won, but an occasional U.S. victory kept the races alive, off and on, until 1964.

Posters like this one from the 1920s drew crowds of up to 70,000 to the lifeboat races. Besides the excitement of competition, the races offered a fine excuse for a picnic and an opportunity to gawk at the city's most important celebrities, such as Mayor Jimmy Walker, who invariably attended.

Ferrying a cadre of Union naval officers across Virginia's James River during the final days of the Civil War, U.S. Marines row a launch with oarlocks cut into the gunwales. These so-called box oarlocks provided the sturdiness preferred on military craft. Other ship's launches are tied up to the double-turreted U.S.S. Onondaga in the background, which was anchored midriver to blockade Confederate traffic.

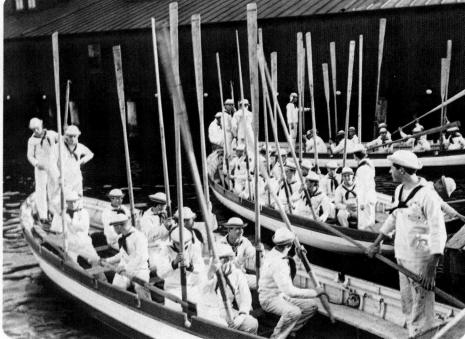

Training to become officers, midshipmen at the U.S. Naval Academy in Annapolis embark for a rowing drill on 30-foot, 12-man cutters. Here, at the coxswain's order to "Up oars," they prepare to set their sweeps in the oarlocks. Skill in rowing was considered so important that the Academy continued these exercises until the mid-1950s.

Oarsmen hold a fishing boat against the current of the Hudson River as commercial shad fishermen haul in their net, tied between poles stuck in the riverbed. The domed structure on the riverbank is the tomb of General U. S. Grant, erected in 1897, only a decade before this picture was taken.

Playing a river bass, a properly suited and hatted angler stands securely amidships in his St. Lawrence skiff, while his guide prepares to net the catch. These skiffs, comfortably fitted with armchairs, were favored around the turn of the century in upper New York State's Thousand Islands. They were quite stable despite their long, narrow hulls, which allowed them to move easily through the water—a trait that endeared them to the guides who did the rowing.

A crew of the U.S. Life Saving Service, forerunner of the Coast Guard, proudly shows off its rescue vessels and equipment, all stowed on trailers or carts for hurrying to wreck sites. Disaster victims were usually ferried ashore in heavy-duty lifeboats (background) or, if the surf was severe, in an unswampable, covered life car (foreground). The carriages at right hold line, flares, lanterns and other rescue gear.

2 In open water on a calm day, handling a powerboat is no more difficult than driving a car across a large empty parking lot. All a skipper has to do is pick a course, engage the gears and throttle ahead. A more representative test of a helmsman's skill comes when he is taking his craft away from the dock or bringing it back in again. These two basic maneuvers, when executed at a crowded wharf on a day of heavy marine traffic, can be downright intimidating, particularly if the tide is running or a wind blows up.

Under these circumstances, a helmsman rapidly discovers that most of the time, driving a powerboat is not at all like driving a car. The differences be-

MANEUVERING UNDER POWER

come apparent as soon as he drops his lines and starts toward open water. A car goes where it is pointed, stops quickly when bidden and can remain stopped indefinitely. A boat, however, once free from land, never comes to a complete standstill until it is firmly tied up again. It is pushed about by wind and current, buffeted by the wakes of other boats. Worse yet, a boat has no brakes. The only way to slow one down in an emergency is to throw the engine into reverse—and even then the vessel's momentum may carry it a considerable distance ahead.

Another deviation from automobile behavior is the fact that a boat steers with its tail. It turns because water forced against the rudder—or in the case of an outboard, the propeller thrust—swings the stern to port or starboard. In response, the bow points in the opposite direction. In open water, where there are no other boats around and plenty of room to turn, this steering idiosyncracy makes little difference. But in close quarters it can make some very negative differences indeed if the skipper neglects to allow room for the lateral swing of his stern or for the sometimes slow response of his bow. On the other hand, an accomplished helmsman can take advantage of his boat's turning peculiarities to jockey it through some fancy pivots and crabwise maneuvers impossible with a car. He can even swing a twin-engine craft around in its own length without using the rudders, as the skipper at left is doing.

Before achieving such mastery, a skipper must come to understand the enormous variations in the way different boats respond to the helm. Each has a different turning radius. Displacement boats do not accelerate as quickly as outboards, but they carry their forward way long after the engine is cut. While a heavy inboard can be stopped by generous use of reverse throttle, the same maneuver might cause an outboard, with its low transom, to back into its own wake, and swamp.

A wise helmsman takes extra time and extra pains to become acquainted with an unfamiliar boat. The first time he takes it away from the dock, he moves cautiously and slowly—and if possible, he invites someone who knows the boat to handle the wheel until he is in the clear. Once in open water he performs a few experimental maneuvers to gauge the vessel's idiosyncrasies. One test is to throw a cushion overboard and practice approaching it from all angles. (This is also a good man-overboard drill.) In putting his craft through its paces, he applies the principles and procedures outlined on the following pages: discovering how propeller and rudder action makes boats behave the way they do, and how balance and trim affect a craft's performance. He learns how much throttle he needs to maintain steerageway, and how much room he should leave for his stern to swing when turning. He begins to assess such things as wind and current by observing how other boats are lying to their anchors. And in time, the feel he gains for his craft's performance prepares him for the ultimate satisfaction of mastering the challenges—such as inlet running (pages 158-159)—that occur in the everyday excitement of boating.

Without touching the wheel, the helmsman at a power cruiser's flying-bridge control panel exploits his twin-engine boat's maneuverability by making a tight turn using throttles alone.

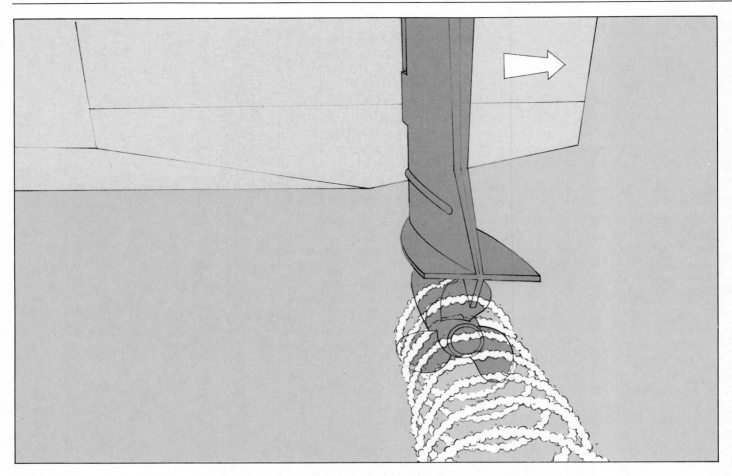

With an outboard motor the boat is steered
by turning the entire engine—propeller
and all. When the propeller swings to the
left, as here, its thrust cone, which is
indicated by the path of bubbles spiraling
out from the blade tips, pushes the stern to
starboard (arrow); the bow in response turns
to port. In reverse the thrust works in the
opposite direction, pulling the stern to port.
In either case the turn could be sharpened
by swinging the propeller farther over or by
throttling up to produce more thrust.

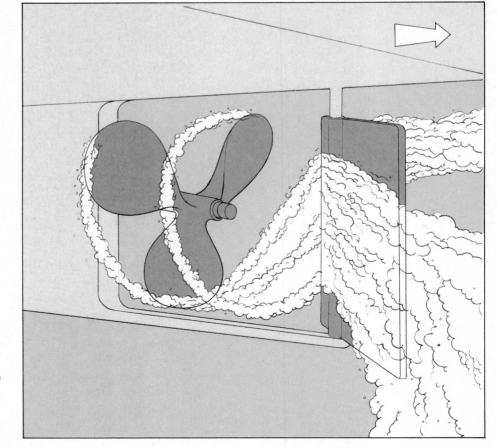

The rudder of an inboard turns a boat by
diverting a part of the propeller's thrust to
either the left or the right. Left helm, as here,
diverts the left side of the thrust cone,
swinging the stern to starboard, while the
right side of the thrust cone continues
to push the boat ahead. With a rudder system
the stern swing is not as forceful as with
an outboard. And in backing, where
the thrust is directed forward, only the boat's
movement through the water acts on the
rudder, making steering difficult (opposite).

The Thrust for Turning

Powerboats turn because of forces generated in the water by either their rudders, the thrust of their propellers or both together. Powering ahead at normal cruising speed, a helmsman brings these forces to bear simply by turning his wheel in the direction he wants to go. When backing down, the helm directions are reversed. Putting the rudder, or propeller, to the right swings the bow to port, while left helm turns the bow to starboard.

When a boat backs down, and even when it is powering forward at very low speeds, a secondary force comes into play. This is the tendency of a propeller to pull sideways in the direction of its spin, as its rotating blades bite the water. That is, a standard "right-handed" propeller, which turns clockwise, pulls the stern slightly to starboard when going ahead. In reverse, the same propeller turns counterclockwise, and so slews the stern to port.

Powerboats with twin engines and twin propellers have no tendency to edge sideways. The two props counter-rotate, thus balancing out their sideways impetus. Twin propellers offer another key advantage: when properly manipulated (below) they can pivot a boat in a full circle within its own length.

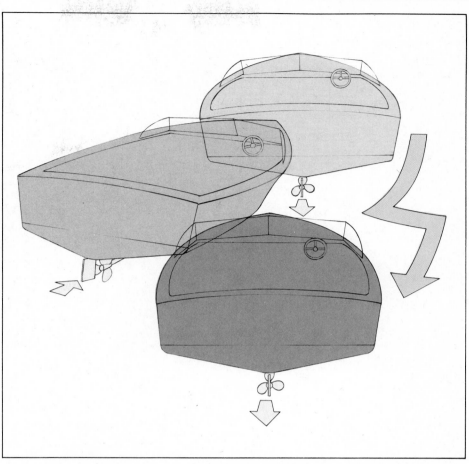

When a single-engine inboard backs down (top) the rotational force of its propeller pulls the stern to port. To correct for this movement, often called port backing, a helmsman applies a quick burst of forward power with the rudder hard left (middle), swinging the stern back to starboard (bottom).

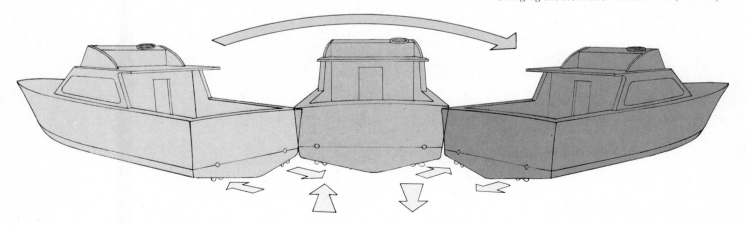

With its starboard engine set in reverse while its port one powers ahead, a twin-screw cruiser swings its bow sharply to starboard in a maneuver that does not use the rudders at all. The engines' push-me-pull-you effect pivots the hull on its stern, without creating any backward or forward movement.

Skidding around a Turn

A tightly circling outboard's broad, spiraling wake reveals the combination of skid and pivot that carries a boat around a turn. The bow, moving a comparatively short distance, produces the white inner half circle. The stern slithers in a wider arc, leaving the two larger wakes emanating from its transom. The turn is of a short radius, because the thrust from the engine, angled to starboard, acts directly to push the stern to port. The hull pivots at a point along its central axis, while sliding obliquely to the side, as shown by the arrow in the diagram at right. If the engine could be at a 90° angle to the transom, the boat would pivot around, with no forward movement at all.

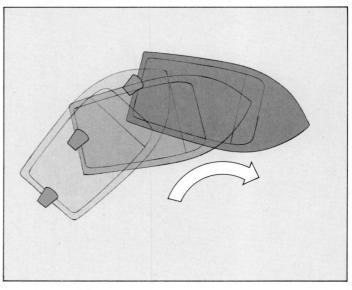

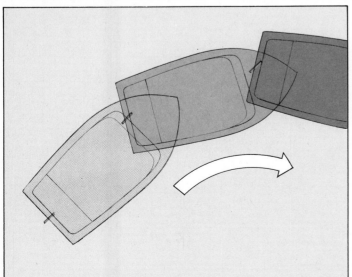

The inboard above is circling as tightly as possible at speed—yet as the diameter of its wake indicates, it cannot turn as sharply as the outboard-equipped boat of comparable size (opposite). Since the inboard's propeller angle is fixed, and its rudder can convert only a fraction of the propeller's thrust into a sideways push (page 50), the stern slips slightly to the side and the hull tends to track more directly ahead (arrow, left). Increasing the inboard's rudder angle beyond the point shown in the diagram will not make the turn tighter; when the rudder angle reaches 40°, it creates so much turbulence in the water moving past it that most of its steering effectiveness is negated.

The Importance of Trim

There is an optimum angle at which every boat should ride in order to move fast, handle best and make the most efficient use of its engine's power. In the high-speed outboard at right, this preferred angle—called trim, or attitude—is shown in the middle picture; the slightly raised bow allows planing without blocking the driver's vision. Poor trim causes a bumpy or sluggish ride and wastes fuel.

One way to adjust a boat's trim is simply to rearrange passengers and equipment until the hull rides properly. There are other ways, however, to produce the same effect. An engine-tilting mechanism (below and right) controls trim by changing the angle of the propeller's thrust. If the bow rides low, the engine can be tilted away from the transom so that the propeller pushes the stern down—thus bringing the bow up. If the stern is low, the engine can be tilted the other way.

On some boats with heavy outboards, a hydraulically controlled tilting mechanism (opposite, top) allows the skipper to fine-tune his trim when the craft is underway. And on large boats—particularly inboards, where the propeller angle is fixed—hydraulic trim tabs (opposite, bottom) sometimes do the job.

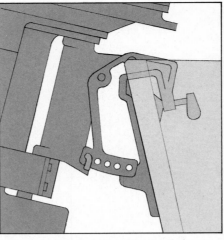

Setting the tilt pin in the aftermost hole may provide proper trim for a bow-heavy boat; but with a boat evenly loaded, this setting can lift the bow too far out of the water (right).

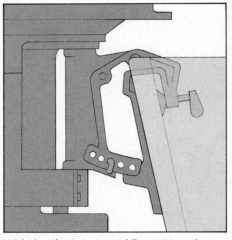

With the tilt pin in its middle position, the engine drives the boat at the proper angle for the conditions shown at right: calm seas and a boat with no passengers or extra gear.

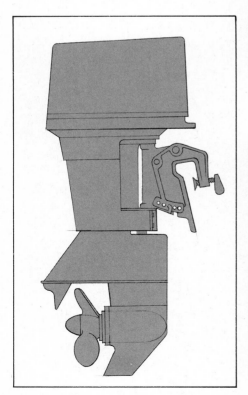

A trimming device on a typical outboard motor is a mounting bracket with holes for a tilt pin. The pin's setting determines the angle between the boat's engine and transom.

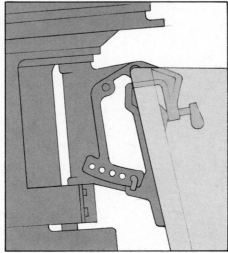

Moving the tilt pin to a forward hole brings the bow of a lightly loaded boat too far down. But with a heavy stern load the position that is shown above would be correct.

A remote-control hydraulic trimming device, often incorporated in large, high-powered outboard engines like the one shown below, allows a helmsman to adjust the engine angle—and the balance of his boat—by a touch of a button on the control panel. Since the skipper can trim while underway he gets a faster, safer and more efficient ride.

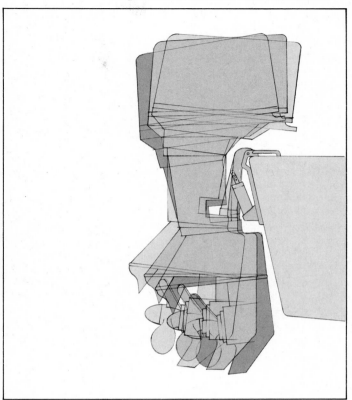

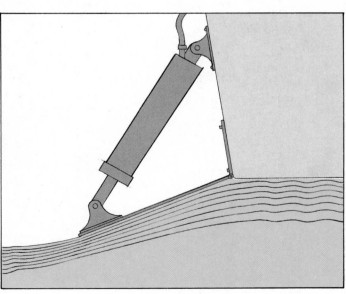

A trim tab on an inboard's transom controls the angle of the craft's stern in the water. Acting somewhat like the elevator on the tail of an airplane, the tab exerts downward pressure on the water rushing past it, thus lifting the stern and preventing it from settling too far as the boat gathers speed. Like an outboard's tilt pin, hydraulic trim tabs can boost a boat's speed and efficiency.

Docking Techniques

The most demanding of day-to-day boat handling situations is the business of maneuvering in and out of docks and slips. Well before he arrives at his berth, the helmsman puts out fenders and readies his docking lines. He also notes the direction of the wind and current; wherever possible, he approaches on the leeward side so that the wind coming out from the dock will slow his advance. The pilot of a single-screw inboard also plans ahead for his departure from the dock; if he has to back out, he will want his starboard side toward the dock to take advantage of his boat's tendency to back to port *(page 51)*.

The photographs on these and the following pages show step-by-step docking procedures for both a single-engine and a twin-screw inboard. Diagrams accompanying each photograph indicate the position of the rudder and the direction the propeller is turning *(below)* during each maneuver. The rudder's angle is shown from the viewpoint of a helmsman glancing over his shoulder toward the stern: that is, when the helmsman applies left rudder, the stylized rudder in the diagram angles to the viewer's right.

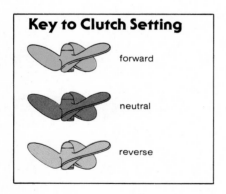

Key to Clutch Setting

forward

neutral

reverse

Coming in to a Dock

To berth his single-screw inboard, the helmsman approaches the wharf at a 45° angle, his engine throttled down. While still a boat length away, he throws the rudder hard to the left, causing the boat to swing its starboard side toward the dock.

Leaving a Dock

Leaving the dock, the helmsman prepares to back out—the usual method in crowded situations. Engine idling, he allows the breeze—its direction shown by the flapping pennants—to push him clear. In a calm, he would shove himself away from the dock.

To keep from hitting the boat ahead, the helmsman shifts the engine into reverse, gives the throttle a short burst, then shifts into neutral. While this maneuver successfully stops the boat, the reverse propeller tends to slew the stern to port, away from the dock.

The helmsman corrects the stern's swing by shifting to forward for a moment so that the propeller thrust against the rudder—still hard left—throws the stern to starboard. Then he shifts back to neutral, and the boat slides gently and precisely into the berth.

Just off the dock, he puts the helm hard left and the engine in reverse so that the stern slews to the left. The turn is accentuated by the propeller's tendency to pull left; to back to the right, the skipper might have to use the method shown on page 51.

Still in reverse, the helmsman works the bow clear of the dock area. As the boat gains sternway, the rudder, now amidships, begins to control it. In a moment the helmsman will shift into forward and turn the rudder to the right to maneuver into the channel.

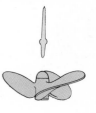

Entering a Slip

Moving slowly as he begins making the 90° pivot required to enter a narrow slip, the helmsman starts turning at least a boat length away. His helm hard to the right, he keeps enough forward throttle for steerageway, while his crew gets the docking line ready.

The skipper momentarily puts his propeller into reverse to stop the boat's forward motion, while the momentum of the turn continues — aided by the propeller's natural tendency to move the stern to the left when backing. The boat lines up for entry.

Backing out of a Slip

As he starts out of a slip, the helmsman looks back to make certain the channel between the docks is clear of other boats. With rudder amidships and the engine in reverse; the propeller's torque swings the stern to the skipper's left as the boat moves backward.

Still moving astern, the helmsman tightens the boat's turn by throwing the rudder to the right, shifting into forward and giving the throttle a brief burst. These actions slow the boat's movement astern, while the rudder helps push the stern harder toward the left.

Starting in, the helmsman shifts from reverse to forward, and noses gingerly into the slip, his rudder held amidships. The boat's new forward movement has made it stop pivoting, though the wake curving from the stern still traces the path of the turn.

Once inside the slip, the helmsman uses one more short burst of power in reverse to bring the boat to a quick and complete standstill before its bow touches the dock. Meanwhile his crew is prepared to make the docking line secure to a cleat ashore.

To get the bow well clear of the slip, the engine is again shifted to reverse with the rudder thrown hard left. This opposite shift of the rudder while the engine runs in reverse keeps the stern moving to the left, helping the boat to complete its pivot.

In the final step of the maneuver, the engine is shifted into forward. As the boat gains headway, the pivoting movement will stop and the boat will settle into a straight course. Fully underway, only slight changes of rudder angle will be required to steer.

Docking with Twin Screws

The helmsman prepares to back a twin-screw cruiser into a slip—a maneuver facilitated by its superior handling qualities. Where a boat cannot come alongside a dock, stern-first docking allows passengers to climb aboard over the wide transom.

When the boat is positioned just outside the slip, the helmsman shifts the right engine into neutral and the left one into reverse, while throwing the rudders to the right. This maneuver both slows the boat and turns the stern toward the entryway of the slip.

Pulling Away

Heading out from its slip, the twin-screw cruiser moves ahead with rudders amidships. Since the boat's propellers spin in opposite directions, they offset each other's tendency to creep sideways. No rudder action is required to straighten the boat's stern.

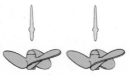

Once the stern clears the slip, the helmsman pivots the boat by leaving the right engine in forward and putting the other in reverse. No rudder is needed to assist the turn—although a little left rudder can be applied, at the helmsman's discretion, for insurance.

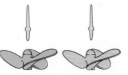

To continue pivoting the hull and lining it up with the slip, the helmsman puts the right engine in forward while leaving the left one in reverse. Even tight turns like this one can be executed so easily with twin engines that little rudder movement is needed.

Properly aligned and with both engines in reverse, the boat backs down straight. If the boat goes slightly askew, the helmsman can swing the stern to the right by backing down with only the left engine; or he can swing to the left by using only the right one.

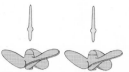

As the bow comes around to the desired heading, the helmsman takes the left engine out of gear and puts the rudders well to the left. With the right engine still going ahead, the boat accelerates forward while the stern continues sliding to the right.

The maneuver completed, the helm is put amidships and both engines are throttled ahead slow, at equal speed. In a narrow channel such as this one, excessive speed will create a wake that would knock neighboring craft against the pilings.

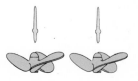

ULTIMATE TEST FOR BOAT AND MAN

No boatman in his right mind would even approach the menacing wall of green water curling above the Coast Guard lifesaving boat at right. But the coxswain at its helm is not only in full control of his mind but also of his boat, as he deliberately stands out toward this 15-foot comber breaking over the bar off the mouth of the Umpqua River in Oregon. As shown here and on the following pages, this virtuoso helmsman is pitting his boat handling skills and intimate knowledge of how his craft behaves under stress against some of the roughest conditions normally found in United States coastal waters.

The coxswain and crew are practicing their technique for reaching small boats trapped among such waves, or people washed overboard in the surf. The aim of the drill is to time the waves so as to plunge straight through a breaker on the way out and to ride one in as would a surfer. The sea is treacherous, however, and in mammoth combers such as these, even the most skillful helmsman sometimes gets caught broadside. Then tons of water cascade across the deck, roll the boat on its beam ends (page 64) and occasionally turn it clear over. For half a minute or more, the crew members may then find themselves trapped under 15 feet of water, lungs straining for air.

Fortunately, this is no ordinary boat nor crew. The round-bottomed craft is designed to roll easily with the punches, and the weight of heavy twin-diesel engines mounted low in the hull quickly brings it rightside up again. When submerged, it ships only a little water through its motor ventilators, and elsewhere none at all. The hatches are all watertight and any seas entering the open cockpit—called the coxswain's flat—flow right out again. The crew members, as rugged as their craft, are prepared day and night to set out after boatmen who were not so well prepared to challenge the sea.

Poised to do battle with a breaking comber off the Oregon coast, a 44-foot Coast Guard motor lifeboat sets out on a training mission that tests to the limit the abilities of craft and crew. More than 100 lifeboats similar to this rugged 16-ton vessel, designed for rescue work in nearly impossible conditions, are in service on U.S. waters.

A Coast Guard lifeboat riding a massive Pacific breaker (above) gets caught in the curl of the wave. In an instant (above right), the force of tons of moving water tosses the boat over on its side. Few other boats—or crews— could survive such punishment, but this one will right itself in about 30 seconds. Its curved foredeck and cabin top will shed most of the water back into the sea; what remains on board flows down quickly through large one-way drainpipes, or scuppers, designed to clear water from the well deck in a hurry.

On another day of breaker drill (right), the lifeboat survives a bone-jarring encounter with a cresting sea and emerges from a cloud of spray under full control, triumphantly cruising at speed along the curl of a wave.

Crash-helmeted crew members, observed in a moment of crisis by a remotely controlled camera mounted behind them, hang on for life as a heaving sea flips their lifeboat on its beam ends. The coxswain, strapped in his chair, guns the engines to give the boat more steering control in fighting through the furious onslaught of the waves.

3 A small boat is a relatively docile, simple and forgiving device. It is less complex, mechanically, than a typewriter, and far less temperamental than, say, a color television set. No prodigious feats of physical strength or coordination are required to control it. And though the safe, efficient maneuvering of any sailboat, small or large, presumes a knowledge of the basic principles described on the following pages, these principles are not difficult to acquire. In fact, some of the nation's best racing skippers taught themselves.

For most beginners, though, a sailboat represents a bundle of barely controllable hazards, ready to dump everyone into the water. Part of the begin-

HOW TO MAKE A SAILBOAT GO

ner's mystification comes from the fact that a sailboat's motive power comes from an invisible and ever-varying force: the wind. Before a sailor can persuade his boat to go where he wants, he must know where the wind is coming from. An experienced sailor instinctively reads the wind's direction from its feel on his cheek, and he can spot an approaching gust by the patch of darker ripples it leaves as it moves across the water. The novice must trust to more obvious signs: bits of yarn tied to the shrouds and the little weather vane (called a masthead fly) at the top of his mast. Or he may look for indicators ashore, such as a flag or smoke rising from a stack. To develop a sense of the wind's direction, the novice should practice at random moments—and not necessarily on the water. For example, he can decide whether he is reaching or running while he walks his dog or lugs his laundry across a parking lot.

At sea on a moving boat, however, the wind's exact direction may become harder to detect. Just as an open car in motion creates the effect of a breeze on its driver, all moving sailboats create their own apparent winds. Thus, sailing into the wind makes the breeze feel stronger—and seems to move its source to a point nearer the bow. Going downwind the opposite happens. The wind seems mysteriously to die, even though the boat may be surging through the water almost as fast as the wind itself.

With each fluctuation, the skipper must move his tiller—and sometimes adjust his sails—to compensate. The tiller is a special source of confusion to most new sailors, since it must be moved in what seems like the wrong direction to turn the boat. Structurally, a tiller is essentially a lever arm that pivots on a fulcrum to change the rudder angle. Pushing the tiller to starboard turns the rudder to the left; in response the boat swings to port. This seemingly contrary behavior of tiller and boat runs counter to the deepest instincts of most beginners, and only practice will make helm movements quick, sure and instinctive: tiller to starboard, boat to port, and vice versa.

Even when they have caught the knack of basic tiller movements, neophyte helmsmen often fall into another fault: they oversteer. By manipulating the tiller too hard and too often, they slow the boat and even impair its maneuverability. Great helmsmen, like fine tennis players, seem to accomplish miracles doing very little; a firm, sensitive hand on the tiller is best.

A third source of worry for most beginners is the tendency of most small centerboard boats to heel over easily. Since there is no heavy keel to hold them upright, any force of wind on most points of sail tends to lay small craft on their sides. The skipper and crew are the only effective ballast. They must learn to shift their weight, according to the wind's direction and force, to keep the boat as close as possible to an upright position—which is its best attitude for sailing.

Even if a sudden gust does capsize the boat, no catastrophe ensues. Most small boats are easily righted *(pages 92-93)*. And turning over, like falling from a horse, is an established milestone in the experience of learning how.

His hand firmly on the helm and his sails trimmed for moving to windward, the skipper of a small racer coaxes his craft along. His crew leans to windward to hold the boat upright.

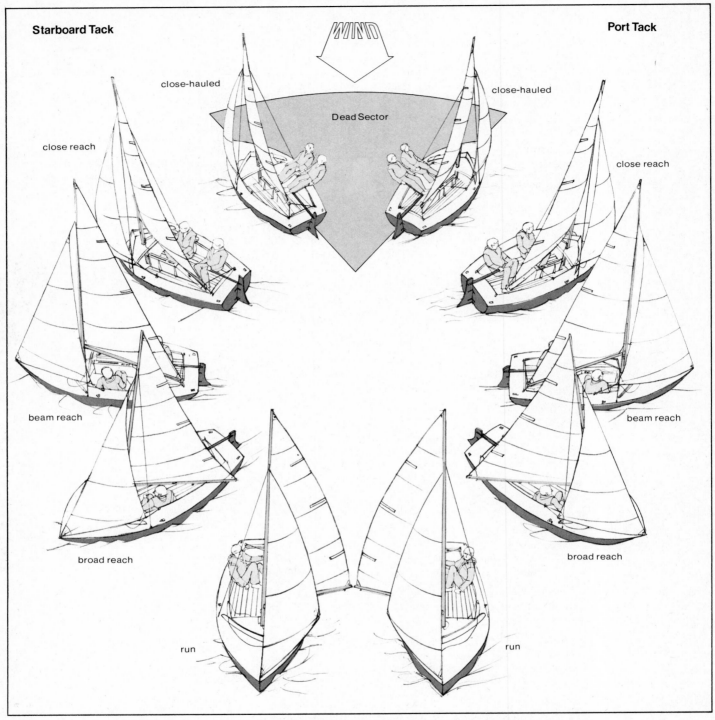

Starboard Tack

Port Tack

WIND

close-hauled

close-hauled

Dead Sector

close reach

close reach

beam reach

beam reach

broad reach

broad reach

run

run

*The basic points of sail are illustrated by the various headings of
these boats; each one is moving in a different direction relative to
the wind. The boats on the right, all on the port tack, are headed
progressively farther off the wind: the boat at top right is close-hauled;
the next three are on various degrees of a reach; the bottom boat
is running. In the sequence at left, each boat is on the starboard tack.*

Points of Sail

The wind is so important to a sailboat that every direction the vessel takes—indeed each motion the helmsman makes with the tiller—must be understood in relation to it. No sailboat can travel directly into the wind, of course. But outside a dead sector extending about 40° to 45° on either side of the wind's eye, a boat can sail effectively in any direction.

The various slants the boat can take relative to the wind are known as its points of sail. When the helmsman trims in his sails and approaches as close to the wind as he can without luffing, he is said to be close-hauled, pointing or beating. If he eases his sails and steers off the wind, he starts reaching—generally the fastest and most comfortable point of sail. When he turns all the way downwind, so that the breeze comes over his stern, he is running or going before the wind.

Besides being specifically divided into close-hauled, reaching and running, the points of sail are split into a pair of generalized categories called tacks. These, too, are directly related to the wind. A vessel is sailing on the port tack when the wind blows against the left—or port—side of its sails; on a starboard tack, the wind strikes the sails on the starboard side.

When one sailor is teaching or commanding another in helmsmanship, virtually all of the orders are linked to wind direction. "Head up" is an instruction to turn the boat more into the wind. "Head down" means the opposite, as do "head off," "fall off" and "fall away"—all of which tell the helmsman to turn the boat farther away from the wind. And as the helmsman performs these maneuvers, he should remember the contrary alliance between his tiller and rudder. To head up he must put the tiller down, to leeward; and to fall away he must point the tiller up, to weather.

On each heading, the skipper and crew must adjust the sails in order to move the craft effectively *(right)*. In a two-man boat like the one shown on these pages, the skipper usually controls the mainsheet, while his crew is in charge of the jib. For beginners the business of trimming sail—indeed, the whole problem of balancing the boat properly and efficiently on the different points of sail—may at times seem mysterious, if not altogether confusing. But if the skipper ever feels he is getting into trouble, all he has to do is let go the sheets and head into the wind. There will be a considerable flapping of sails, but the boat will stop while all hands pull themselves together to begin anew.

When a boat is close-hauled (left), or else reaching (center), its sails act as airfoils. Thus, while the sails in these two illustrations are trimmed at different angles to the boat, they are set at a nearly constant angle to the wind to create an efficient aerodynamic flow. But when a boat is running (bottom), the wind simply pushes against the sails from behind, sharply reducing the aerodynamic effect. Furthermore, the mainsail may blanket the jib, i.e., prevent the wind from reaching it. Some skippers, therefore, carry their mainsail on one side and their jib on another, as here—known as sailing "wing and wing."

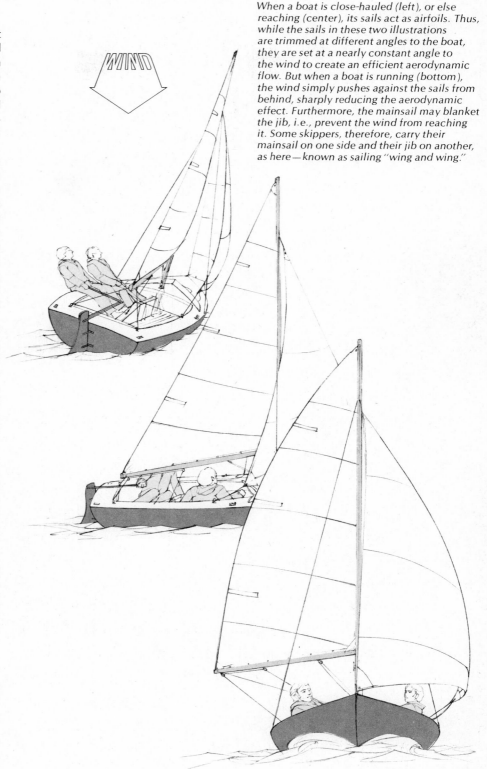

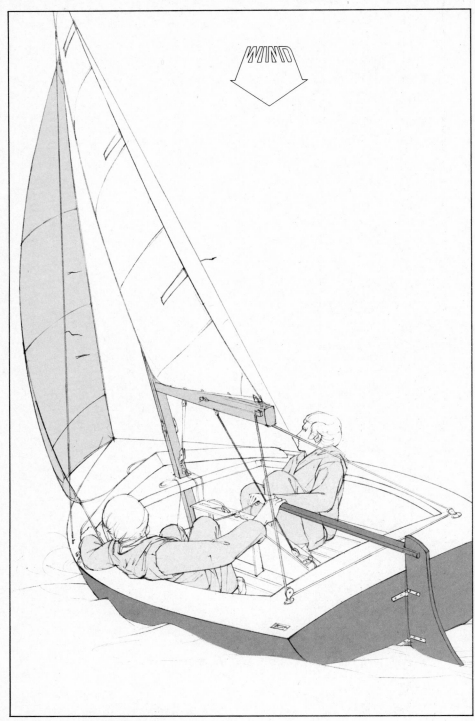

Properly trimmed and balanced to sail upwind, this boat has both jib and mainsail pulled in tight, with the boom approximately over the transom's leeward corner. The tiller is nearly centered and the centerboard is fully down. In light air, the skipper may sit to leeward, as here, so he can watch the jib for signs of a luff. In moderate to heavy air, he would be sitting to windward.

Going to Windward

Sailing into the wind is a form of nautical brinkmanship. The boat moves in a delicate balance between wind and water, tipped toward one side, the helmsman steering as close to the wind's source as he can while keeping his sails full. Every shift of the wind's force or direction, no matter how subtle, affects this balance, and to redress it the helmsman must move his tiller and shift his weight.

The helmsman sets his course by the wind. Both jib and mainsail are sheeted in tight and kept there, as in the picture at left. On a small boat the sheets are either held by hand or secured in quick-release cam cleats; if a surprise gust heels the boat too far over, they must be let out in a hurry to bring the hull upright.

Once his sails are strapped down firmly, the helmsman makes sure he is heading as close to the wind as possible by constantly testing his course *(opposite)*. If he heads too high, or "pinches," the sails lose most of their pulling power; speed drops, the helm feels sluggish and if the boat moves the slightest bit closer to the wind, the jib will begin to luff. To correct this, the helmsman turns away from the wind—but not too far, or the sails will again lose power. Most of the wind's force will tend to heel the boat over rather than drive it forward.

In tightroping this narrow line at the wind's edge, the helmsman must keep alert to continual changes in the wind's velocity. Puffs will heel the boat, possibly bringing in water over the rail, and the skipper and crew will have to hike out to keep the boat balanced. Or the breeze can disappear suddenly, so that they will have to hurry inboard again.

A fluctuation in the wind's strength also brings a change in its apparent direction *(page 69)*. A gust tends to move the apparent wind aft, allowing the boat to point higher for a moment without luffing. A drop in the wind in effect moves the breeze toward the bow, forcing the helmsman to fall off temporarily to leeward.

An experienced helmsman can sense these changes in the wind almost instinctively, from the boat's angle of heel, from the changing patterns of ripples on the water's surface to windward or from the feel of the water against the rudder, transmitted to his hand via the tiller. He studies the leading edge of the jib, the first place to luff when the wind moves forward. And as an additional aid, he may attach telltales to his shrouds and sails that will instantly signal the most sensitive shifts in the wind's flow.

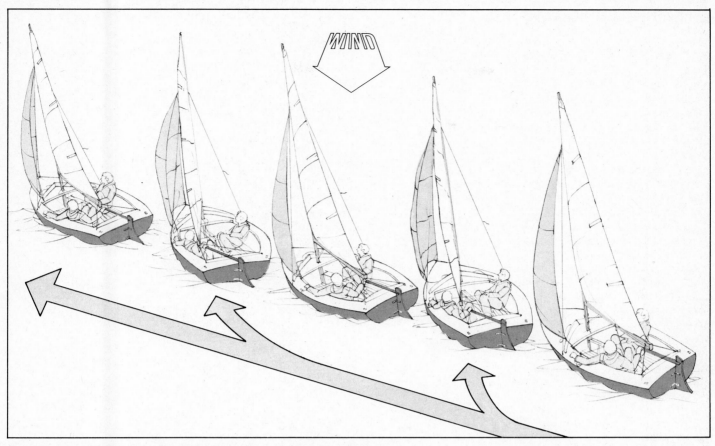

A system for testing course in order to sail as close to the wind as possible is illustrated here. To make sure that the wind has not shifted or that he has not inadvertently strayed too far downwind, the helmsman keeps nudging his tiller a few inches to leeward to see if he can head a little higher. If the jib begins to luff, he quickly heads back down to the original course. If not, he continues edging upwind until he is on the verge of a luff, falls off a fraction to pick up speed and sails along on his new heading.

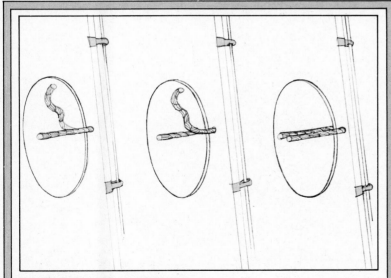

A Sophisticated Telltale

The traditional telltale is a piece of yarn tied to a shroud to indicate wind direction. Many racing boats now use another kind of telltale as well, one that records the flow of air across a sail, as shown here. It consists of a yarn threaded through the jib near the luff, so that the ends hang out on either side of the sail. The sail cloth between is replaced by a small window of transparent plastic so that both yarns are visible (on small boats where the sail is often thin enough to see through, no window is necessary). If the boat falls away too much, air eddies make the leeward telltale flip up or down *(left)*. When the boat heads too high, the windward telltale flutters *(center)*, showing that the jib is about to luff. When the two yarns are parallel, the airflow is balanced and the jib is drawing perfectly *(right)*.

Technique for Tacking

Often, when a boat sails close-hauled, the skipper is trying to reach a point so close to the wind's source that he cannot head directly for it. He must approach his destination in a series of alternating tacks, following a zigzag course like the one at right. In effect, he is climbing up the wind, much as a railroad train climbs a hill in a series of switchbacks.

Each time the helmsman changes tacks, he swings the bow of his boat through the wind's eye. This procedure, called coming about, requires close teamwork between the skipper and crew and is accompanied by a set of verbal commands, described on the opposite page.

As the bow turns into the wind, the sails will luff and the boom will swing from one side of the boat to the other; skipper and crew will have to duck their heads to avoid getting hit. As the boat's momentum carries it around, the crew must release one jib sheet and take in the other at precisely the right moment. If the crew faults his timing, or if the boat is traveling too slowly to complete the turn, it may simply fall back on its old tack, a situation called "missing stays." Or worse, it may hang, shuddering, head to the wind and then drift helplessly backward (page 77), a predicament known as "being in irons."

An experienced helmsman will not only avoid these blunders, but can actually gain ground to windward by adroit steering; instead of slamming the tiller to leeward, he moves it firmly but gradually, sailing the boat through the tack. He also knows how to time his tacks to get the most mileage to windward for the least amount of hard sailing. When his destination is dead to windward, and there are no strong currents to set him off course, he makes tacks of roughly equal duration.

But he watches closely for a wind shift that may help him along. If the wind moves more abeam, allowing him to head higher without luffing, it is said to be giving him a lift toward his mark; he rides the lift as long as he can. If the wind moves toward his bow, the shift is called a header; and he must fall off in order to keep his sails full. But a header on one tack becomes a lift on the other, and if the skipper comes about as soon as he feels the shift, he may find that the wind has given him a free ride home.

Such dividends from close attention to the wind's vagaries are one of the real rewards of sailing. But an inexperienced or inattentive skipper and crew occasionally find themselves in one of the difficulties on the following pages.

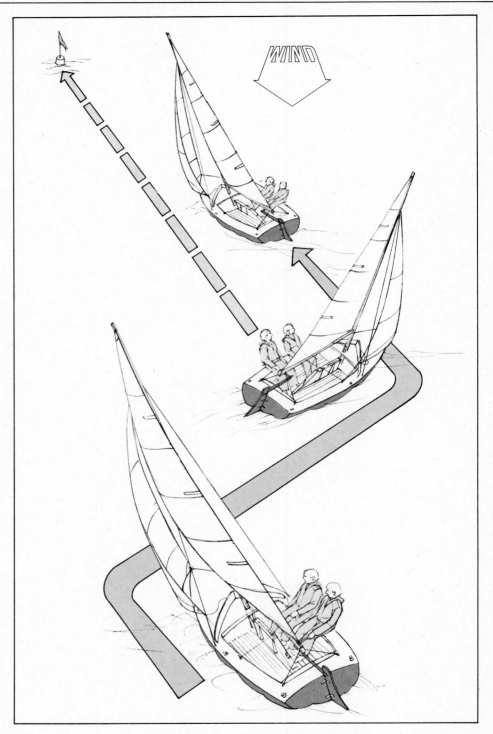

Beating to windward, the skipper of this boat must follow the zigzag course shown by the blue arrow to reach his goal. To cut his distance over the water, he sails each leg as close to the wind as he can. He prepares for his final tack when the mark is at right angles to the center line of his boat (dotted arrow)—or directly behind him as he sits facing across the boat. Then, waiting a moment to allow for the boat's tendency to sideslip when sailing upwind, he comes about to head directly for—or fetch—the mark.

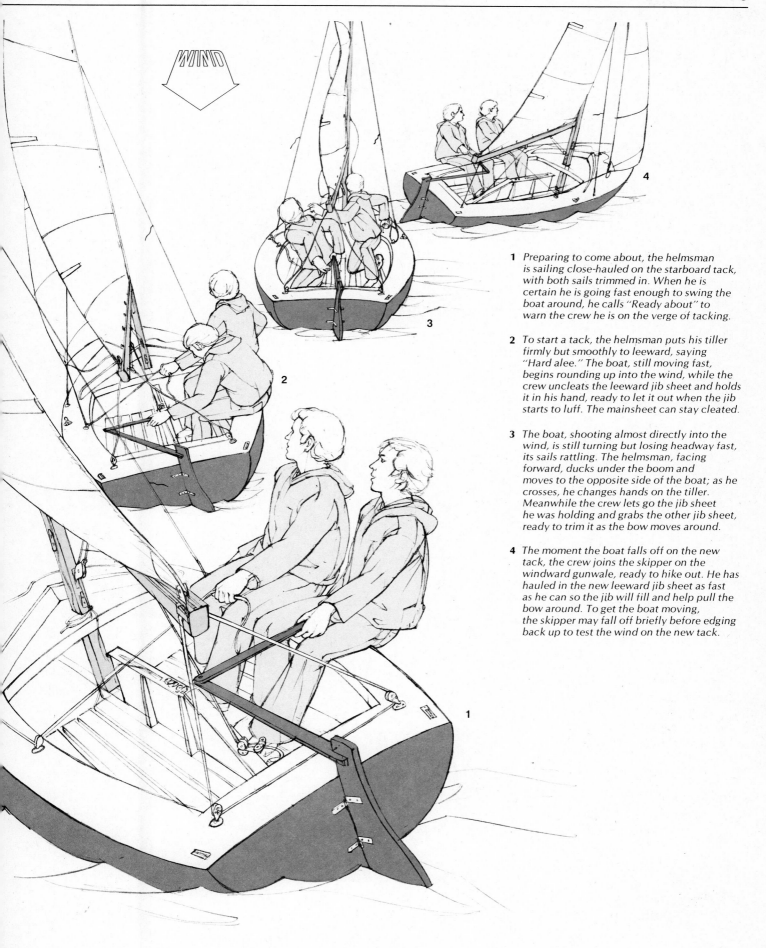

WIND

1 Preparing to come about, the helmsman is sailing close-hauled on the starboard tack, with both sails trimmed in. When he is certain he is going fast enough to swing the boat around, he calls "Ready about" to warn the crew he is on the verge of tacking.

2 To start a tack, the helmsman puts his tiller firmly but smoothly to leeward, saying "Hard alee." The boat, still moving fast, begins rounding up into the wind, while the crew uncleats the leeward jib sheet and holds it in his hand, ready to let it out when the jib starts to luff. The mainsheet can stay cleated.

3 The boat, shooting almost directly into the wind, is still turning but losing headway fast, its sails rattling. The helmsman, facing forward, ducks under the boom and moves to the opposite side of the boat; as he crosses, he changes hands on the tiller. Meanwhile the crew lets go the jib sheet he was holding and grabs the other jib sheet, ready to trim it as the bow moves around.

4 The moment the boat falls off on the new tack, the crew joins the skipper on the windward gunwale, ready to hike out. He has hauled in the new leeward jib sheet as fast as he can so the jib will fill and help pull the bow around. To get the boat moving, the skipper may fall off briefly before edging back up to test the wind on the new tack.

One typical tacking problem occurs when the crew trims the jib too soon. Here the crew has sheeted in the jib before the bow has crossed the wind. The wind fills the jib from the wrong side, or backs it, forcing the bow back toward its original heading.

Letting the jib go too late, after the bow has moved through the wind, also puts the jib aback. While in light airs an instant of backing can help turn the bow onto its new heading, the crew must let go the jib quickly, or the boat will turn too far and slow down.

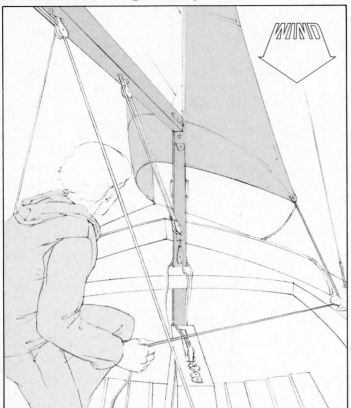

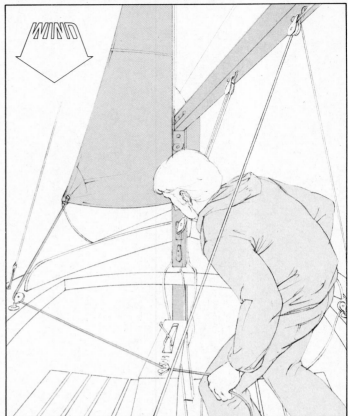

Tacking Troubles on a Tall Ship

Compared to a modern sloop, old-fashioned square riggers were very inefficient at beating to windward: They could sail no closer than 60° to the wind, as opposed to a sloop's 45°. Thus, while a sloop sails only about 14 miles over the water to gain 10 miles to windward, a square rigger would have to sail close to 20 miles to reach the same goal. The square riggers were so inefficient when beating that they often had to stay anchored in port for days until they had a fair wind to get them out to sea.

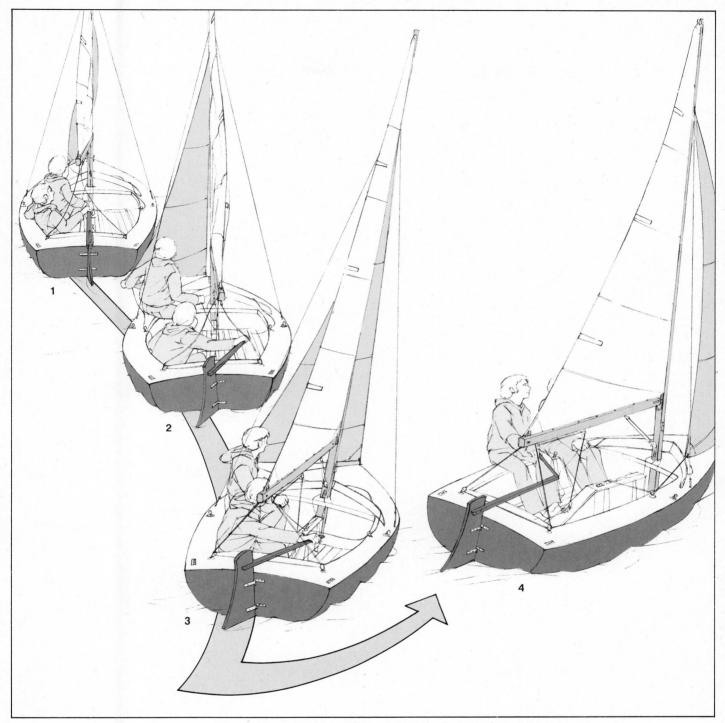

Getting out of irons after a failed tack can be maddeningly difficult
for a novice who has not mastered the corrective action shown
here. At top left the boat is caught head to the wind and lies
dead in the water (1). To come out of irons (in this case on the port
tack), the skipper tells the crew to hold out the jib to port (2),
backing it so the wind will drive the bow to starboard. As the boat
drifts backward, the skipper reverses his helm, pushing the tiller
to starboard; this swings the stern to port (3). As the mainsail fills,
checking the boat's backward drift, the helmsman puts the tiller
amidships (4) while the crew lets go the jib and sheets it in to
starboard. Soon the boat will be well underway on her new tack.

In trimming a boat for a reach, the skipper first sets his course directly for his mark. Then both sails are eased out to the first sign of a luff, and quickly trimmed back a few inches until they fill completely. The helmsman sits to windward where he can see ahead and still watch the mainsail, and where his weight will help balance the boat. In light airs the crew may sit to leeward, where he can keep a close watch on the jib and be ready to sheet it in the moment it starts to luff.

Reaching and Running

In reaching and running, unlike tacking upwind, the helmsman need not zigzag to his objective; he simply picks his mark and heads for it. The wind on a reach comes anywhere from 35° forward of the beam to 35° behind it; and the sails should be trimmed just short of a luff, as described at left. Now, since the helmsman is not trying to work his way along a narrow line at the wind's 'edge, he can keep his helm steady; instead of responding to each wind shift with the tiller, he trims and retrims his sails to maintain their correct angle to the wind.

When reaching, the skipper and crew must also make constant adjustments for fluctuations in the wind's strength. Each puff increases the boat's tendency to heel, and its occupants must be ready to sit out to windward—or hike out—in order to keep the craft as level as possible. In an especially strong puff that heels the boat over hard, the skipper can ease the wind's lateral pressure by easing out the mainsheet and momentarily turning his vessel downwind. This tactic puts the boat onto a more even keel and gives it a brief boost in speed while it rides out the puff.

On a run, with the wind coming over the stern, the sails are let out until they are set roughly perpendicular to the wind—although the mainsail should not be eased so far that it presses against the shrouds. Once the boat has settled on its course, moving along with the wind, the breeze seems to drop. Since there is no lateral pressure on the sails, the boat loses most of its impulse to heel, and the crew need not hike out. The craft's tendency to slide to leeward also disappears, and the centerboard can be raised to reduce underwater drag. (On a reach the centerboard may also be hauled up, though only partway, as shown at right.)

Despite the relaxed feeling of sailing on a run, all hands must remain alert, for at any moment a following wave may swing the stern off line and an inattentive skipper may find himself headed in a totally unexpected direction. Furthermore, with the apparent wind decreased, the direction of the true wind becomes harder to detect. It may unexpectedly shift more abeam, requiring that the sails be trimmed to compensate. Or it may shift unnoticed to the same side of the boat on which the mainsail is being carried. This creates a dangerous situation known as sailing by the lee, and unless the skipper quickly heads up, the wind may catch the sail on the wrong side and slam it across the boat in an accidental jibe.

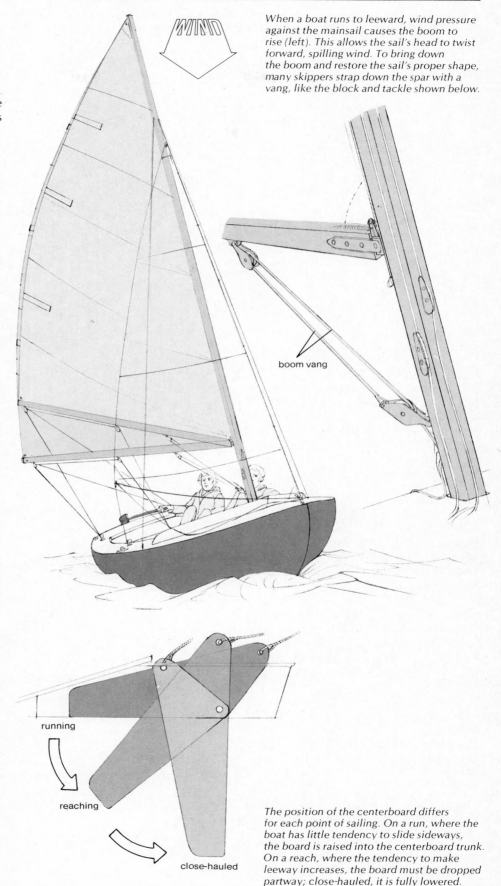

When a boat runs to leeward, wind pressure against the mainsail causes the boom to rise (left). This allows the sail's head to twist forward, spilling wind. To bring down the boom and restore the sail's proper shape, many skippers strap down the spar with a vang, like the block and tackle shown below.

boom vang

running

reaching

close-hauled

The position of the centerboard differs for each point of sailing. On a run, where the boat has little tendency to slide sideways, the board is raised into the centerboard trunk. On a reach, where the tendency to make leeway increases, the board must be dropped partway; close-hauled, it is fully lowered.

Jibing under Control

Heading downwind, whenever a helmsman changes tacks he executes a maneuver called a jibe. In so doing he moves the stern of the boat through the path of the wind and brings the mainsail from one side of the vessel to the other. Simple as this tactic sounds, it requires even closer timing and coordination than coming about. For unless the boom is properly guided, it can swing across the boat with alarming suddenness and immense force, knocking down anyone who forgets to duck. Or it may lift up and snag on a stay, sometimes tearing out fittings or capsizing the boat. Also, unless the helmsman minds his tiller, the momentum of the jibe may swerve him wildly off course.

If properly controlled however, as at right, a jibe presents none of these hazards. To start a jibe the mainsail should be sheeted all the way in to reduce the path of its swing. Then, with the main thus trimmed, and the stern to the wind, the slightest movement of the tiller will suffice to bring the wind into the other side of the stern, and start the boom across. A helmsman can anticipate the boom's swing by watching the jib since, when a boat is running downwind, the jib provides early warning of an imminent jibe by flapping lazily and then swinging across to fill on the other side. The boom will follow seconds later.

When the boom does cross, the helmsman must slack off the sheet as quickly as possible. Otherwise the force of the fast-swinging, wind-filled sail will tend to pivot the boat broadside to the wind—a perilous occurrence called broaching (*opposite, top*) which can end in a capsize. To reduce the chance of a broach, the helmsman moves the tiller no more than is absolutely necessary to turn the boat; and he anticipates the boat's tendency to round up broadside by angling the tiller back for a moment toward his original course as though he were getting ready to jibe again in the other direction. Then, the danger past, he steers his new course.

In light airs, wind pressure against the sails is sufficiently gentle so that the hazards and complexities of jibing are reduced. Often the helmsman can ignore the sheet entirely; the crew simply grabs the boom and heaves it across the boat.

In moderate to heavy wind, however, quick action and close timing are vital. One trick for ensuring a safe, easy jibe is to wait until the boat has picked up speed from a passing gust. Then, as the boat moves faster, the apparent wind will drop and the sails will be easier to handle.

Jibing from the starboard to the port tack, the skipper of the boat above first announces the impending maneuver by calling "Ready to jibe." Then, at the command "Jibe ho," he puts his helm over, turning the boat from a broad reach to a dead run (1). When the stern begins moving through the wind (2), he hauls in the main sheet. The moment the boom crosses the boat (3) the helmsman lets out the sheet; the crew trims the jib as the boat settles on the new tack (4).

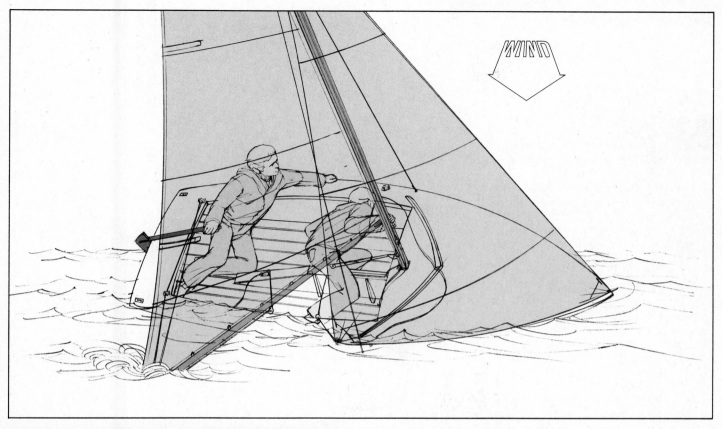

A careless jibe in which the skipper did not mind his steering has caused this boat to broach dangerously. As the hull swings beam to the wind, pressure in the sails lays it over on its side, burying the tip of the boom in the water. The dragging boom end prevents the skipper from letting out the mainsail farther; the lifting hull has pulled the rudder partly out of the water so the boat no longer responds to the helm. Though the helmsman and crew scramble to shift their weight to windward, water is already coming into the cockpit and a capsize is imminent.

A Free-wheeling Jibe

Very small sailing craft such as Sunfish and Lasers respond so quickly to the wind that they require a special technique for jibing. If the sail is sheeted in during the jibe, as it would normally be on a larger boat, the helmsman might not then be able to let it out fast enough to prevent a broach. Therefore he simply gives the sheet a tug to start the jibe, and lets the boom swing freely across and all the way out on the other side.

Setting a Chute

Few sights in sailing are more thrilling than the billowing shape of a wind-filled spinnaker. But the real beauty of the spinnaker is as much efficiency as looks: no sail moves a boat along with more authority on any point of sail from a beam reach around to a dead run.

Spinnakers, or chutes as they are sometimes called, are a bit more complicated to put up than any other sail. But by preparing the sail in advance and by following a methodical procedure while rigging and hoisting it, a skipper and crew can raise a spinnaker in a matter of seconds.

Preparations begin on land, where the spinnaker is carefully folded into either a sail bag or a cardboard box *(right)*. This precautionary step cuts down the risk of snags or twists when the sail is hoisted. On board the boat, the spinnaker sheets must be rigged so that they go outside all the boat's shrouds and stays, thus allowing the chute when set to fly high and clear of all other rigging.

To rig the sheets properly, first they must be led through blocks on the stern near the rail. When they have been passed outboard of the standing rigging, their forward ends should be clipped together and placed on deck just forward of the leeward shroud. Then the bagged or boxed spinnaker is set down beside the clipped ends—to leeward, where the blanketing effect of the mainsail and jib will keep the spinnaker from filling prematurely with wind and perhaps blowing overboard before it is fairly set.

Just before the sail is hoisted, the sheets are unclipped from each other and fastened to the two bottom corners of the sail. The halyard, which leads through a block high on the mast just above the headstay, should be checked to make sure it runs free. Then it is led outside the jib sheets and clipped to the sail's head.

Finally, the spinnaker pole, which holds out the windward corner of the sail, is put up. The windward spinnaker sheet slips into a fitting at the pole's outboard end; thus fitted, the sheet is called a guy, and for efficient trimming, it may lead through a guy hook on deck. The topping lift—a halyard for the pole itself—fits onto the middle of the pole. The pole's other end is snapped to a ring on the mast. Now the sail is ready to set.

On a small boat manned by two people, the helmsman trims the guy and sheet *(opposite)*, while the crew hauls up the sail, cleats the halyard and drops the jib. On a larger boat, as many as half a dozen crew or more may share these complex tasks.

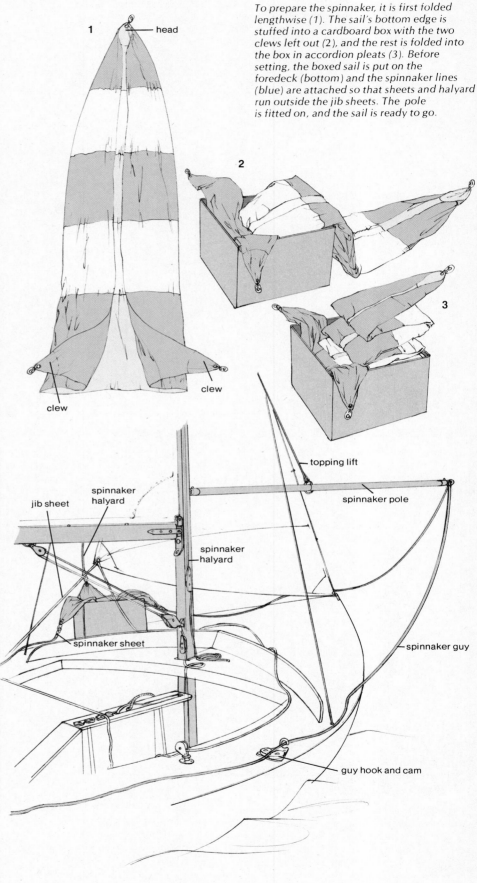

To prepare the spinnaker, it is first folded lengthwise (1). The sail's bottom edge is stuffed into a cardboard box with the two clews left out (2), and the rest is folded into the box in accordion pleats (3). Before setting, the boxed sail is put on the foredeck (bottom) and the spinnaker lines (blue) are attached so that sheets and halyard run outside the jib sheets. The pole is fitted on, and the sail is ready to go.

1 — head

2

3

clew

clew

clew

topping lift

spinnaker pole

jib sheet

spinnaker halyard

spinnaker halyard

spinnaker sheet

spinnaker guy

guy hook and cam

As the spinnaker is hoisted, the helmsman holds the boat steady downwind, steering with the tiller between his arm and his side to leave his hands free. (Many sailors stand with the tiller between their knees.) While the crewman hauls fast and hard on the halyard, the skipper controls the sheet in one hand and pulls back on the guy with the other. When the spinnaker is all the way up, the crew cleats the halyard, lowers the jib and then moves aft to take over the sheet and guy for adjusting the spinnaker's trim on the run downwind.

Flying a Chute

The spinnaker, once it is aloft, works best when flown as high as possible. There the breeze is steadiest and the sail pulls hardest. Keeping the chute airborne requires constant trimming of its sheet and guy to adjust to changes in the wind's direction. This job belongs mainly to the crew.

First the crew trims the guy, which controls the position of the spinnaker pole. When the wind moves aft, the pole should also be pulled aft; thus, if the boat is on a run, the pole will stick out abeam. When the wind shifts forward, the pole should be angled forward, so that on a beam reach it may almost graze the forestay. With the guy properly set, the crew plays the sheet, easing it out until the sail's windward edge begins to curl, then edging it back in. A major wind shift will require adjustment not only of the sheet but of the guy (opposite page).

The helmsman and crew who can set and trim a spinnaker need learn only two more spinnaker-handling skills—how to jibe the chute and how to take it down, operations described on pages 86-87.

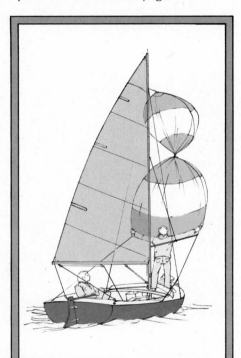

The Untimely Hourglass

The bane of all spinnaker handlers is the hourglass, which occurs when the sail gets twisted on itself, as shown above. This often happens just after the sail has been raised, before it has been brought under full control. To straighten the sail, the crew eases the halyard a bit and pulls down on both edges of the sail. The twist should rise up the sail and vanish.

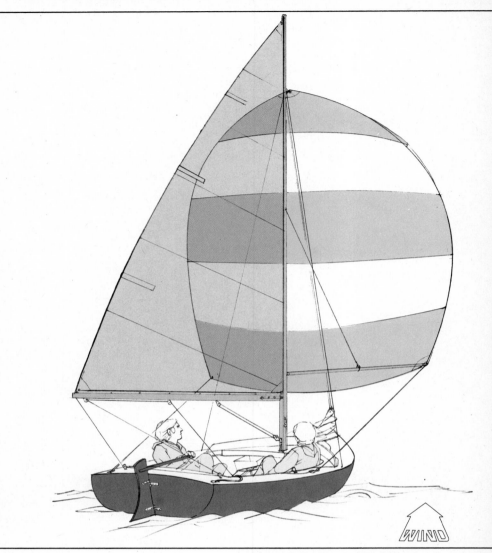

Perfectly trimmed and pulling hard, the spinnaker above rides high up and ahead of the boat, presenting a full, unruffled surface to the wind. The tack and clew are level with each other and the spinnaker pole is horizontal. The sheet is eased well out, allowing the sail to lift forward to a point just before the sail's windward edge begins to curl. Both skipper and crew sit aft to compensate for the fact that the pull of the chute, exerted high up on the mast, tends to tip the boat forward and bury the bow.

WIND

A wind shift forward has brought a curl to the luff of the spinnaker; unless proper trim is quickly restored, the sail may lose still more wind and collapse entirely. To refill the chute, the crew pulls in the sheet (arrow) until the curl disappears; he may then ease out the guy so the spinnaker pole swings slightly forward, putting it at the proper angle to the new slant of wind. The helmsman can help by bearing away slightly, bringing the wind aft to fill the sail while the crew trims, then edging back to his original course.

If the spinnaker pole is too far forward and the sheet is trimmed in too tightly, the chute will be blanketed by the mainsail and it will start to collapse. To bring the spinnaker out from behind the mainsail and fill it with wind, the crew hauls in the guy (arrow), bringing the pole aft until it is at roughly right angles to the apparent wind. Then the crew slacks off the sheet, setting the chute in a new position relative to the new angle of wind and lifting it out ahead of the boat, where it draws best and pulls hardest.

Jibing a Chute

When jibing with a spinnaker, both the mainsail and chute are brought from one side of the boat to the other. Announcing "Ready to jibe," the skipper tucks the tiller under his arm and takes charge of the spinnaker sheet and guy, playing them to keep the sail full. As the helmsman holds the boat steady downwind, the crew unclips the spinnaker pole from the mast and hooks its free end to the sheet, as shown above. Since the line from the sail's windward corner is called the guy, this sheet becomes the guy on the new tack.

Dousing a Chute

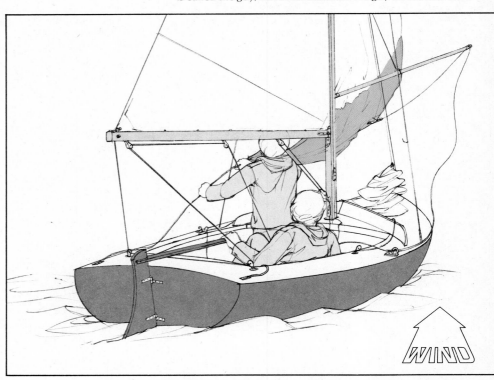

To lower the spinnaker the crew grabs the sheet as close to the clew as he can. Holding the sheet in one hand, he reaches over to the cam cleat and releases the guy, letting it run free through the fitting at the end of the spinnaker pole. As the sail moves behind the mainsail it spills its wind, and the crew hauls it in under the main boom (above). He then drops the halyard (above, right) and pulls down the sail. Finally he takes down the spinnaker pole and stows it.

At the command "Jibe ho!" the skipper brings in the mainsail and eases onto the new tack; the smaller his course change, the easier it will be to keep the spinnaker full. At the same time the crew unhooks the spinnaker pole from the original guy, now called the sheet, and secures the pole's free end to the mast (above, right). The crew then slips the new guy under the guy hook on the windward side and releases the new sheet from the leeward guy hook. He takes over the sheet and guy from the skipper and plays the sail on the new tack.

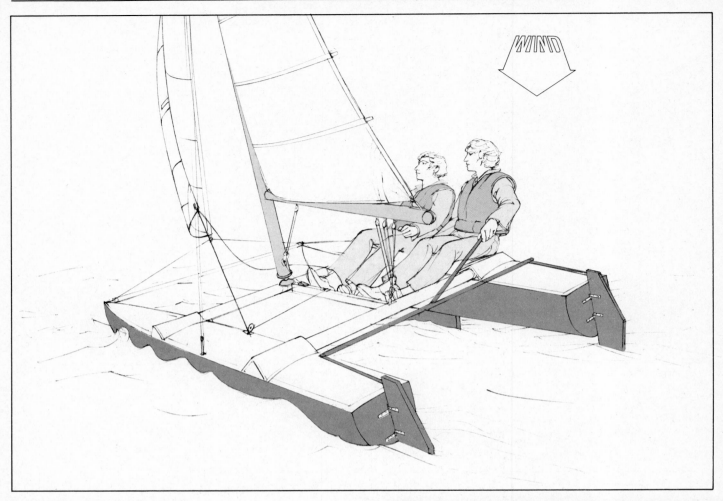

Heading to windward at an angle of about 50° to the true wind, this catamaran is sailing in its most efficient attitude. The sails are sheeted in and the crew has balanced the boat at an optimum angle to the water. Its windward hull is just out of the water, reducing drag, but its centerboard stays immersed to resist leeway. Some skippers allow the windward hull to rise high over the water, but such a tactic—though impressive— is likely to bury the leeward bow in a wave, slowing the boat and inviting a capsize.

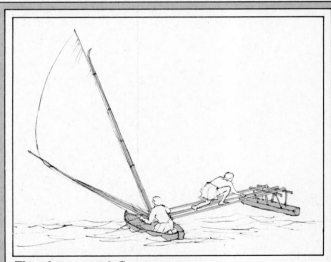

The Ancestral Catamaran

An ancestor of the modern catamaran is the outrigger canoe, or proa, that has been sailed for centuries by the seafaring peoples of the Pacific. A double-ender that always carries its outrigger to windward, the proa reaches effortlessly, but is cumbersome to work upwind: when it changes tacks it must be turned end for end (the bow becoming the stern) so that the outrigger remains on the windward side. Nevertheless, proas are fast, light and seaworthy, and have carried their navigators across thousands of miles of open ocean, from one end of the Pacific to the other.

Taming a Cat

Why does a catamaran sail faster than the single-hulled boat? The reason is twofold. The cat's twin hulls provide a stable platform capable of supporting considerably more sail than a monohull of equal length could carry, yet the catamaran is much lighter. The result is greater speed. One 32-foot D-class cat has been clocked at more than 35 miles per hour.

This combination of high speed and special design calls for special handling techniques. The cat's headlong motion is so great that it brings the apparent wind farther forward than on a slower craft. So the cat's sails should generally be trimmed in quite close, even on a reach.

Reaching is a catamaran's most efficient point of sail, in fact; at high speeds, the underwater shape of the twin hulls provides lift like that of a hydrofoil. When a skipper is sailing for a windward mark, he should steer a course about 50° from the true wind—a very close reach—to get that extra speed. If he tried to point as high as a monohull would, his speed would drop significantly, and although he might make fewer tacks, he would take longer to reach the mark.

The catamaran's great efficiency on a reach also calls for special downwind tactics. Sailing at an angle to the wind, a cat will go much faster than it will when sailing dead before it. Therefore most cat sailors tack downwind when headed for a leeward mark; that is, they zigzag across the direct course, jibing from broad reach to broad reach and gaining more in speed than they give up in distance (right).

Tacking downwind can be effective for monohulls too, but catamarans, being faster, are more likely to benefit from the maneuver. Also, catamarans are easier to jibe than monohulls. Their great beam gives them tremendous stability and eliminates most of the danger of capsizing or broaching that often afflicts monohulls when jibing.

Cats are somewhat less handy, however, when it comes to tacking upwind. Their light hulls lose headway quickly when pointed into the wind, and because of their width they do not pivot as a monohull does. A cat must therefore be sailed gradually through the wind's eye when coming about; the tiller should be put to leeward only about 20° at first, then should be angled more sharply when the bow comes into the wind. Even when well sailed, a cat will sometimes not carry its way through a tack. Then the jib must be backed, as in getting out of irons (page 77), to bring the bow around.

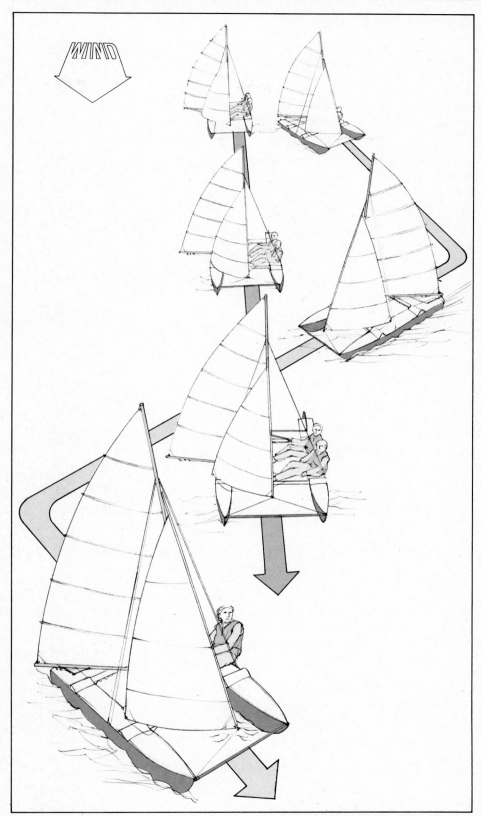

Zigzagging in a series of jibes, a catamaran tacks downwind, outspeeding another cat sailed directly before the wind. The former is going so much faster that its speed more than makes up for the extra distance. The course that gives the most speed for the least extra distance is at about 135° from the true wind, or 90° from the apparent wind.

Mooring and Docking

Few maneuvers are more satisfying to a helmsman than that of bringing his boat up to a dock or mooring with such precision that his crew can step casually ashore with the bow line in hand—or reach with ease for the mooring float as the bow gently nudges the buoy.

The principle to remember in all such maneuvers is to head into the wind while some distance away and coast home, letting the wind act as a brake. The trick is to gauge the boat's momentum—different for every craft at every speed—against the slowing forces of wind or current. The skipper also has to watch out for sudden gusts or lulls in the breeze and be prepared to compensate for them.

Generally, picking up a mooring *(right, above)* is easier than landing at a dock. A mooring usually has more open water around it and allows an approach from any direction. A skipper who finds he is nearing the buoy too fast usually has room to go past it and try again. Sailing on by, incidentally, is better than trying to grab the buoy on the fly, a maneuver that can yank a crew member out of the boat. Should the boat's momentum give out just short of the mooring, a skipper can indulge in some discreet sculling with his rudder by swinging the tiller back and forth. This tactic, though it is frowned on by purists and outlawed in racing, may be just enough to boost the boat the last few yards to the mooring buoy.

Landing at a dock can be as easy as shooting for a mooring if the wind is blowing along the dock or away from it *(bottom, near right and center)*. But if the wind is blowing onto the dock, the skipper has a problem. In this situation the wind will not act as a brake, but will shove him into the dock. Furthermore, it usually is impossible to let the sails out far enough to luff in the wind without having the boom sweep across the dock, banging into bollards or other obstructions.

The solution illustrated below at far right works well in light to medium air. If the wind is really blowing—and it is really necessary to bring the boat in to the dock—a more radical solution may be called for. Sometimes the best move is to drop an anchor some boat lengths upwind from the dock, using the anchor line to back gently downwind to the dock.

The skipper above approaches his mooring on a reach and finally, when several boat lengths to leeward, comes up into the wind. With his sails luffing, he coasts toward the marker, relying on momentum to carry the boat the last few yards. As soon as the crew has picked up the mooring buoy and is securing the mooring line to the bow cleat, the skipper goes forward to lower the sails.

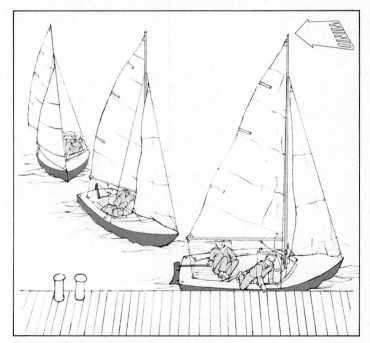

To make a landing when the wind is blowing parallel to the dock, the skipper above approaches on a beam reach, his sails luffing slightly to reduce his speed. He then turns into the wind, spilling the wind from his sails. The boat's momentum carries it gently to the dock as the crew fends off if necessary.

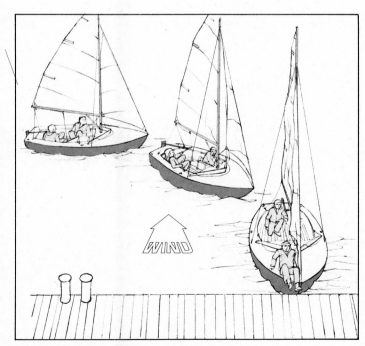

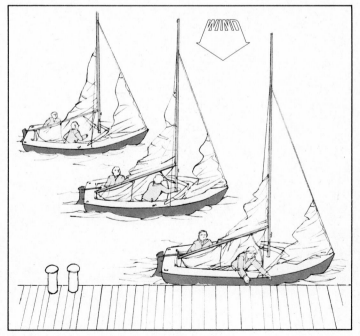

With the wind blowing directly from dock to boat, this skipper sails parallel to the dock on a beam reach, then turns into the wind to slow his craft as it approaches the dock head on. A crew member on the foredeck, hanging on to a cleat or the headstay for stability, extends his feet to fend off the boat.

With the dock directly downwind, one option a skipper has is to round up and drop his sails while some distance upwind, as in the drawing above, and let the wind carry him broadside down to the dock. He should not attempt this maneuver, however, in anything more than light to medium winds.

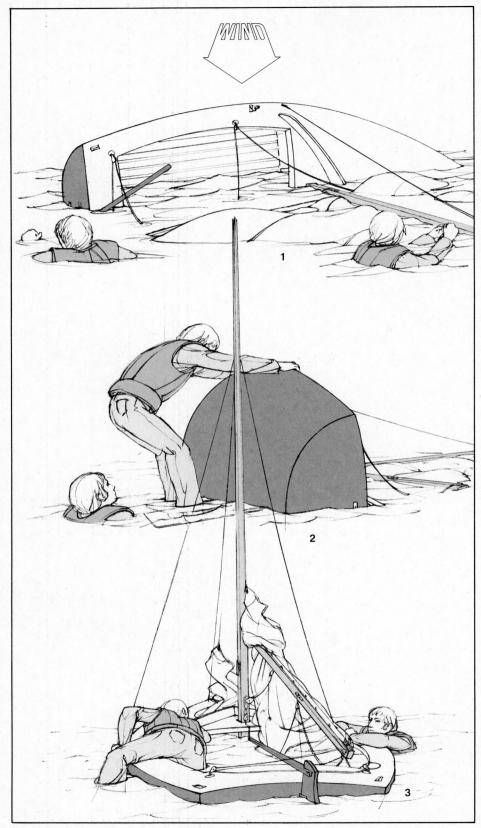

WIND

1

2

3

The two sailors above begin righting their capsized boat by pulling down the sail (1) and pushing the bow into the wind. Next, the skipper stands on the centerboard (2), grasps the gunwale and leans back, levering the boat upright. He climbs aboard and begins bailing (3), while the crew balances the boat.

Over and Up

The term "capsize" suggests disaster to many beginners, but tipping over is not necessarily either dangerous or embarrassing. The best sailors frequently capsize when racing small boats in strong winds, and at some sailing schools, boats are deliberately turned over to teach novices how to handle such a mishap.

The oldest rule for the crew members of a capsized boat is still the best: Stay with the boat. Most small sailboats will float even when filled to the gunwales with water; not only will the boat support the crew members so they do not get tired, but an upturned hull will draw more attention than a swimmer's head bobbing in the water. The record shows that the people who run the worst risks after capsizing are those who try to swim to land.

Sailors who stay with the boat, moreover, have a good chance of righting it. Many small, light craft are designed to float so high when capsized that they come back upright and ready to sail away with a minimum of bailing. Even boats that fill up with water when tipped over can often be put to rights by the method shown at left. Turning the bow into the wind before righting it reduces the chance that a wave will knock the boat back over again; it also puts the boat in the best position to receive a tow. Lowering the sails while the mast is still in the water is also important, for even a small sail holds an enormous weight of water and makes righting difficult.

A righted boat can sometimes be bailed dry, especially if there is a bucket aboard and the crew has plugged the centerboard trunk with a shirt or a sailbag to keep water from coming through. But if waves slop over the gunwales faster than the crew can bail, the boat will need a tow.

Slightly different tactics are called for in righting a catamaran (*right*). The crew must be quick to prevent the boat from going all the way over; when a cat is turned upside down, its mast can stick into a muddy bottom, and in any case it is extremely difficult to right again. Unlike a monohull, a cat should be angled broadside to the wind, since wind against the trampoline stretched between the hulls can help right the boat. But the cat does have a couple of advantages in a capsize: it is so wide that when it comes back up there is little danger of its going over again; and once righted, with its sails still raised, it is set to go. So ready is it, in fact, that the skipper must promptly free the sheets and take control quickly to keep his craft from racing off and abandoning him.

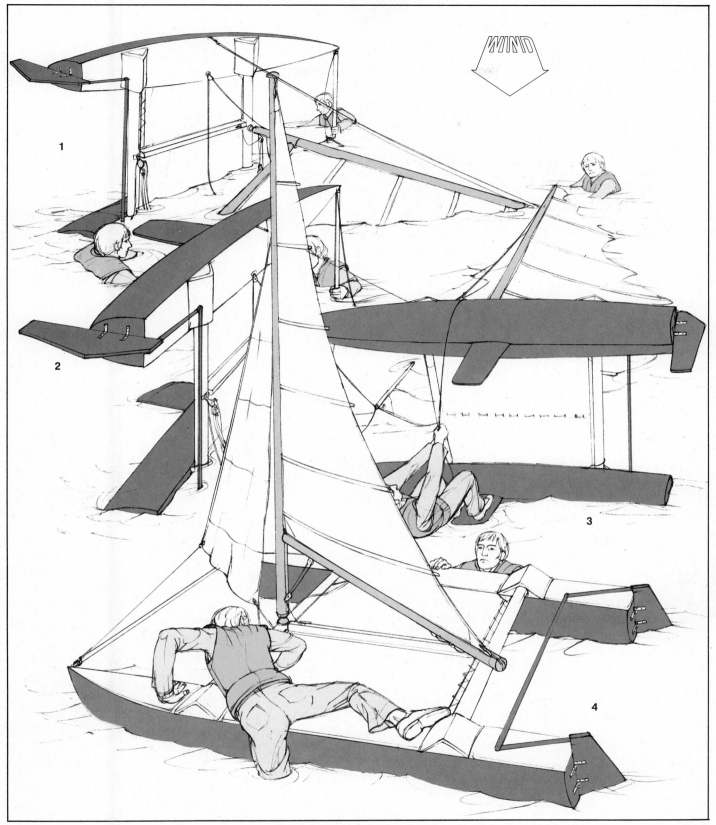

The skipper of a capsized catamaran swims to the bow (1) and starts
turning the boat broadside to the wind (2) while his crew swims
out to the masthead to keep the mast from sinking. Then the skipper
stands on the lower centerboard (3) and leans back on a righting
line (kept tied around the mast), which he has flipped over the upper
hull. Aided by wind pressure on the trampoline, he brings the boat
upright and then climbs aboard (4) as the crew balances the boat.

THE EXCITEMENT OF BIG-BOAT SAILING

Some fortunate boatmen, having mastered basic sailing techniques in small boats, have an opportunity to move up to the challenge of handling larger craft like the 44-foot racing sloop *Gem* seen at right. In so doing they can enjoy the special excitement of sailing in blustery winds that would send a prudent small-boat skipper scurrying for home. Built to withstand the fiercest weather, and equipped to stay on the water for weeks on end, boats of 30 feet and over nevertheless maneuver according to the same principles that govern the movements of a 12-foot sailing dinghy. Yet the differences between small and large sailboats are sufficiently dramatic to demand new techniques and a very different dimension in equipment.

Everything about a large boat is bigger, heavier and more difficult to control. Where a dinghy will luff quickly to a stop when headed into the wind, a large boat may coast a dozen times its own length before stopping—perhaps with a sickening crunch against the dock. Aboard such a vessel masts can reach up to 100 feet above the deck. A spinnaker pole can extend to more than 30 feet and weigh as much as 200 pounds.

To meet the varying wind conditions, big boats may carry half a dozen genoa jibs and spinnakers of different sizes. When the breeze blows up, the tension on the sheet of a big genoa can reach 2,000 pounds. But in strong winds the crew can switch to a smaller jib and reef the mainsail, that is, lower it partially and secure the slack along the boom.

It takes a lot of willing hands to perform these chores, even when aided by muscle-saving winches. Having bunk space for crew enough, ocean racers can keep moving around the clock. When a boat like *Gem* leaves the harbor it can return after only a few hours of hard driving, as on the following pages, or it could keep right on sailing across an ocean.

Boiling along in a 20-knot breeze, Gem slips down a wave during a
gusty sail on Long Island Sound. The crew has just jiffy-reefed
the mainsail, lowering the sail and tying down its new tack and clew,
but not fully securing the folds of excess sail along the boom.

Hoisting the mainsail, a crew member cranks the winch with one hand while guiding the wire halyard with the other. As on most large boats, the mainsail is pulled up with a reel winch, which works like the reel on a fishing rod to wind up and store the halyard.

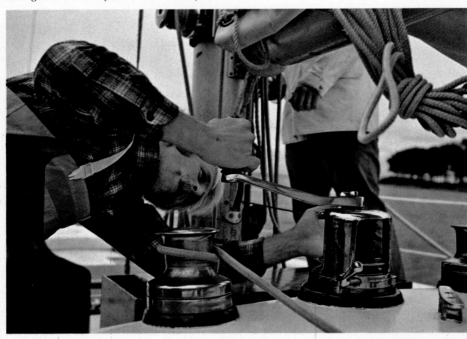

The drum winch that raises the genoa jib calls for two crewmen to operate it: one to crank the winch handle, the other to tail—that is, haul in the slack as the halyard comes off the winch. The halyard is not stored on the winch; it is coiled on deck.

With the breeze piping up, Gem's crew winches up the genoa as the skipper heads into the wind to make the job easier. Anticipating a strong blow, the skipper has selected a heavy Dacron genoa; the line hanging from the boom is used for reefing the mainsail.

Coming about, Gem swings her bow through the eye of the wind. Tacking on a large boat requires precise coordination among crewmen, who frequently must guide the genoa between the mast and headstay to keep it from catching in the rigging.

As Gem completes her tack, the crew hauls in the genoa. Three deckhands are needed to trim the sail in a strong breeze—two to wind a large drum winch and one to tail.

With Gem heeling over in the freshening breeze, the crew sits along the weather rail. Their weight, however, has only a minimal counterbalancing effect. More important is the fact that they have reduced sail by reefing the main and hoisting a smaller genoa.

With the boat now turned downwind, two crew members fetch
a spinnaker from the forward cabin. The spinnaker has been folded
into the bag so that its corners are accessible and so that the sail
will rise smoothly when hoisted. After rigging the spinnaker pole, a 19-
foot aluminum spar stowed along the rail, the crew will attach
the halyard to the sail's head, and the guy and sheet to the clews.

The quickly hoisted spinnaker fills with wind while two crewmen
on the foredeck gather in the genoa jib, which is lowered to keep it
from interrupting the flow of wind into the spinnaker. Gem
has set a so-called star-cut spinnaker, a comparatively small, sturdy
chute used because a fuller spinnaker would be too difficult to
handle. The sail's name comes from the distinctive pattern of its
panels, which are cut to minimize stretch in strong winds.

Plowing downwind, Gem moves along with mainsail eased and the
reef shaken out to present as much sail area as possible to the
wind. Extra sail area in this case is no problem since wind coming
from astern does not heel the boat. A boom vang—the canvas strap
attached to a system of blocks—preserves the shape of the main
by keeping the boom from rising. The genoa lies loosely furled
on the deck, ready for hoisting when the spinnaker is lowered. Gem's
spinnaker pole is tethered down by a foreguy, a line attached to
the underside of the pole and running through a block on the bow.

With the spinnaker down, a genoa set once again and a reef taken in the main, Gem boils through the trough between two waves. Even in blustery weather, crew members on a well-trimmed vessel find time to relax — and even make themselves comfortable — while the boat heads toward home.

4 In days not long past, a mariner could roam for weeks on end, rarely sighting another craft, free to think of nothing but water, wind and the surging power of his vessel. Now all too often that exhilarating sense of freedom is blotted out by the looming presence of another boat, perhaps one as formidable as the giant tanker bearing down on the runabout at left. With the enormous increase in both pleasure craft and commercial vessels—some 900,000 new boats are launched each year in American waters—the boatman today must be as alert to traffic as is any shore-bound motorist. In fact, chugging across such heavily traveled waterways as Puget Sound, Lake Mendota, Wisconsin

THE RULES OF THE ROAD

or Chesapeake Bay has become the nautical equivalent of maneuvering down Hollywood Boulevard on Saturday night. For example, in 1974 two unlighted powerboats, out for a two a.m. ride on a Pennsylvania lake, collided at high speed. The larger boat sank, but its lone operator swam safely ashore; the skipper of the smaller boat was killed on the spot. In Buttermilk Channel, off New York City, an 18-foot powerboat was sliced in two by a towing cable between a tugboat and a barge. Although they were properly lighted, the pilot of the powerboat mistakenly decided that the tug and the barge were not connected. He and his three passengers paid for his mistake with their lives.

Such accidents take more than 1,300 lives and injure nearly 1,500 other victims each year in the United States. The statistics would be infinitely grimmer but for a compendium of laws, commonly called the Rules of the Road, which govern maritime traffic all over the world, and cover almost every conceivable kind of nautical confrontation.

Rules governing nautical conduct have been around for a long time. But their universal acceptance is surprisingly recent and by no means complete. The earliest known set of rules is the Rhodian Sea Law of the Third Century B.C. This dealt principally with damages, salvage rights and punishment for brigandry. These problems still exist, but in modern times the major menace to safe navigation has become—and remains—collision.

England and France in the mid-19th Century formalized the first modern rules aimed at preventing collisions and standardizing nighttime warning lights. Amended in 1889, they became The International Regulations for Preventing Collisions at Sea. And today they are law on the high seas.

Within the United States and its territories, other sets of regulations control water traffic. The Great Lakes Rules govern those inland seas and their tributaries. Western Rivers Rules cover most of the rivers of the central United States. Inland Rules, the most widely used, apply to all other inshore waters and most harbors, river mouths, sounds and bays. (A map of each code's jurisdiction is on pages 166-167.)

The Coast Guard has added to each of the major Rules a set of Pilot Rules, for regional situations. Finally, racing rules govern sailboat competitions.

An aspiring boatman should learn his way through these complexities to ensure his own and others' safety, and to avoid not only physical but financial damages. A boatman who treats the Rules casually may find himself in the shoes of the runabout skipper on Barnegat Bay who ignored a vessel's warning signals and damaged two boats under tow: he was fined $500.

The common boating situations illustrated on the following pages cover major points set forth by the various Rules and explain some of the more confusing differences among them. In all cases the Rules themselves are intended to supplement and reinforce the basic rule of common sense, which is every sailor's best guideline, and which he should follow whenever he finds himself confronted by two conflicting rules—or by another boat.

Prudently waiving his right of way over the huge vessel approaching on his left, an imperiled powerboat skipper applies the rule of common sense and guns his craft out of danger.

Collision Courses: Power

At least 30 per cent of the regulations set forth in the Rules of the Road are aimed at telling the boatman precisely what to do to avoid collisions. The drawings on these and the following six pages illustrate the most common of potential collision situations, and show how the Rules work to prevent disaster. Because most crack-ups involving U.S. boatmen occur in waters under the jurisdiction of the Inland Rules of the Road, the examples and regulations shown are taken from that code, except where otherwise noted.

In almost every waterborne confrontation the Rules designate one vessel as having the right of way; this privileged vessel is required to maintain its course and speed (indicated by arrows on these pages). The other boat is known as the burdened vessel—tinted on these pages—and it must get out of the way. Its best course is also indicated by an arrow. The judgment as to which boat is burdened is based on a concept of relative position, sometimes referred to as zones of approach (below).

In addition to taking proper action, powerboats in potential collision situations must signal their intent with blasts of a whistle, horn, or other sound signal. These warning sounds are of three kinds: long, of 8 to 10 seconds' duration, to be used when leaving a dock or going around a bend; prolonged, 4 to 6 seconds, for use in fog; and short, 1 second, used to signify (and acknowledge) intent to turn right (one blast) or left (two blasts), or to go into reverse (three blasts). A series of short blasts warns of danger.

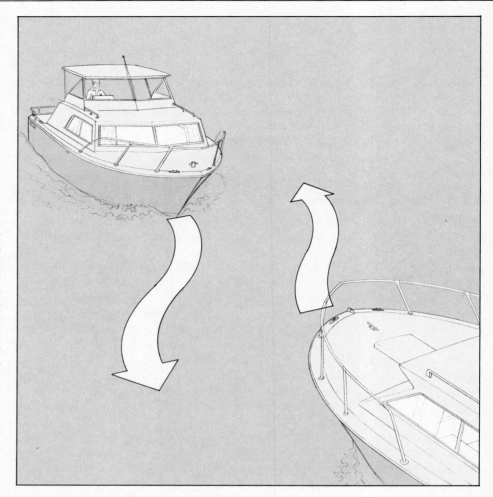

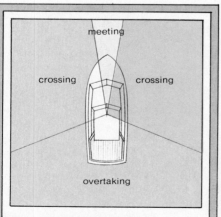

Zones of Approach

Rules of the Road divide the water around a boat into zones of approach. If another vessel appears in a boat's meeting zone or in its right-hand crossing zone, the latter must give way.

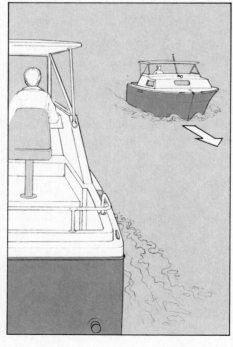

In a potential nose-to-nose collision, each boat is in the other's so-called meeting zone. Therefore both are burdened, and must give way. The Rules state they should turn so as to pass port side to port side, as cars do on the highway. A single, short whistle blast signals this maneuver; giving a similar short blast is the proper response of assent.

Sometimes in a meeting situation, such as the one at left, when two boats are approaching starboard bow to starboard bow, but far enough apart so there is no danger of collision, they can legally pass each other starboard to starboard. Each acknowledges the situation and intent with two short blasts.

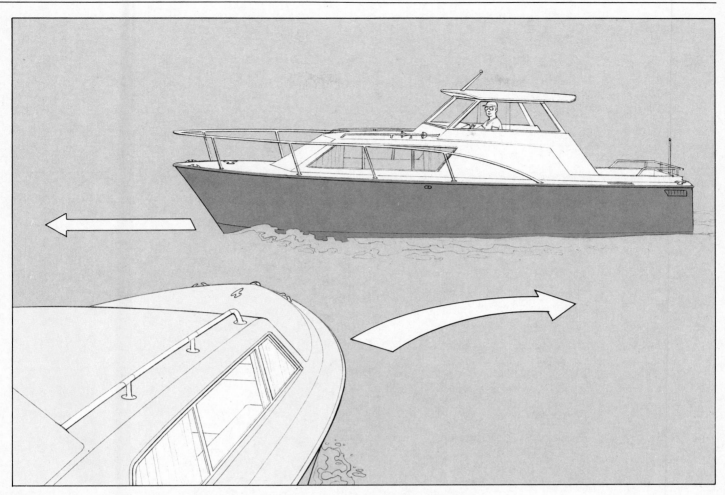

In the crossing situation shown above, the boat in the foreground has the other in its danger zone, i.e., on the right-hand side. No whistle signals are required, but as the burdened vessel, the foreground boat must get out of the way of the other—best done here by turning right. The privileged boat must maintain its course and speed.

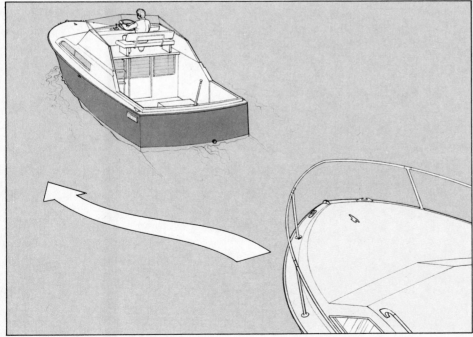

A boat that is overtaking another from behind is always burdened and must stay clear. The usual course is to signal two short whistle blasts, turn left and leave the other boat to starboard. The overtaken boat replies in kind—or if there is danger ahead, warns the other to wait with four short blasts.

Collision Courses: Sail

When two close-hauled sailboats converge, starboard tack always has right of way. The boat on the port tack (i.e., with the wind coming over its port side) must stay clear —by turning to pass astern of the other (below), by tacking onto a new course or by luffing up until the other has passed by.

Starboard tack also has right of way when two sailboats running before the wind on opposite tacks are converging on the same point. However, should one boat approach another from behind, as here, it then is overtaking and must keep out of the other's way regardless of which tack it is sailing on.

In normal meeting and crossing situations, sail has right of way over power. Exceptions occur when a sailboat overtakes a powerboat —and therefore must keep clear— and when the sailboat meets certain power vessels that are operating with limited maneuverability (page 111). A sailboat under auxiliary power also loses its privilege over powerboats even if the sailboat's canvas is hoisted.

When two boats are sailing along side by side on the same tack, the boat to leeward—the one farthest from the source of the wind—has the right of way. The boat on the windward side must avoid bearing down on the other, even if that means luffing up or coming about to the other tack to keep clear.

On inland waters an exception to starboard tack right of way occurs when the boat sailing before the wind on the starboard tack meets one close-hauled: the craft running free must give way even if the other is on port tack. This rule is a relic of the days of square riggers, which were hard to maneuver upwind.

An International Variant

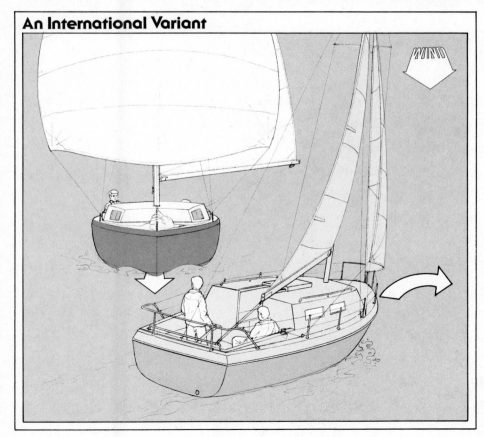

Under International Rules a sailboat on the starboard tack has the right of way even when it is running free and encounters a boat close-hauled on the port tack. This overall privilege to the starboard-tack boat (except when it is overtaking) is also accorded to sailboats in competition under the racing rules of the North American Yacht Racing Union.

Intrusions on the Fairway

A boat moving in a channel—or fairway—normally has the right of way over all boats leaving a dock or berth. The docked powerboat shown below must give one long whistle blast before backing—and must stop if the boat in the fairway warns of a collision by sounding four or more short blasts.

A ferryboat is the only vessel that enjoys the right of way when docking or moving out into the fairway. Though no formal regulation specifies this privilege, the ferry's inherent need to embark and dock repeatedly and on schedule has resulted in a tacit agreement among seamen to give ferries the right of way.

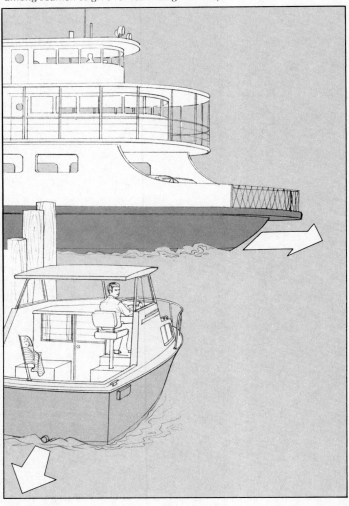

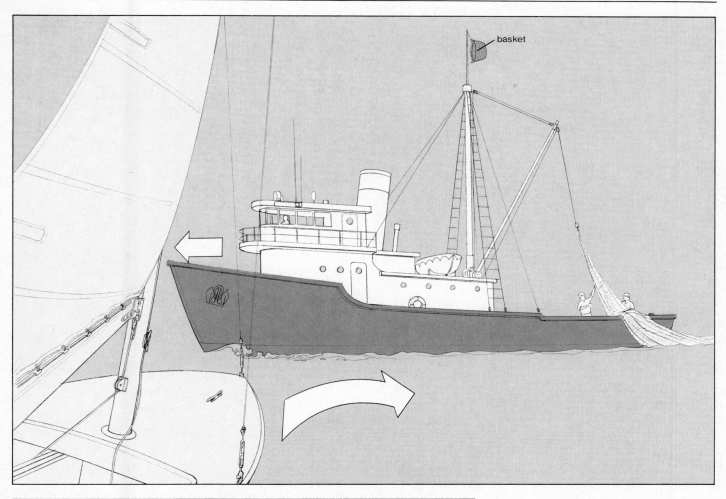

basket

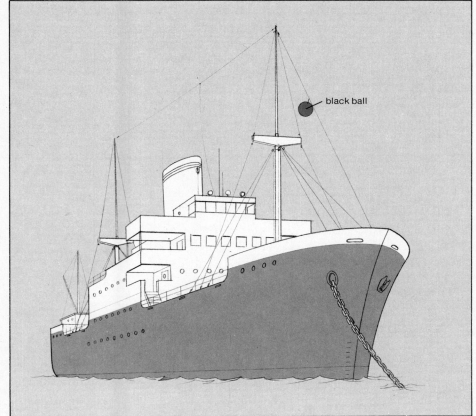

black ball

A fishing boat that is using lines, nets or trawls must display a so-called day shape (see below) in the form of a basket, warning other vessels to keep clear. Under both Inland and International Rules, a sailboat has no right of way over such a fisherman and, as shown here, must turn aside for him. The same rules ban fishing craft from obstructing fairways or channels regularly used by other boats.

Between sunrise and sunset, Inland Rules require a vessel of over 65 feet anchored in a fairway to hoist into its rigging a black sphere at least two feet in diameter. Called day shapes, the sphere and the basket shown above are among several conformations hoisted in daylight to identify vessels with limited or no maneuverability, and to warn other boats to keep clear of them.

The two powerboats, above, approaching each other at a bend in a river, are following the prescribed procedure of keeping well to the right of midchannel whenever practicable. Upon approaching a bend or curve that obscures visibility, a powerboat must signal with one long blast of its whistle when within half a mile of the bend. Any boat approaching from the other side must answer with a similar blast, confirming its presence. When in sight of each other the two will exchange passing signals.

The launch in this illustration is turning to the right, out of the channel and out of the way of an approaching freighter. In so doing the boatman is obeying a very sound canon which specifies that a powerboat under 60 feet long may not hamper the passage, in a channel, of a larger, less maneuverable vessel whose draft forces it to stay in the channel. The larger vessel may also display a day shape in the form of a black cylinder as an indication of limited maneuverability.

black cylinder

Narrow Passages

Though the perils of the stormy sea are legendary, well over half of the boating accidents in the United States occur on lakes, canals and nontidal rivers in perfectly clear weather. The reasons for this unhappy situation are two: the enormous number of small pleasure craft that ply such waters and the fact that a sunny day is a beckoning invitation for everybody to set sail at the same time. Thus the crowded inland waterways on a bright morning are potentially more dangerous to a boatman than a night squall at sea, and navigation in narrow channels, where maneuverability is limited, can be a perilous undertaking—as shown in the illustrations on these pages.

To prevent accidents in these heavily trafficked channels, the various Rules of the Road cover almost any situation a navigator is likely to encounter. However, some of the differences among the four sets of Rules can cause accidents if not thoroughly understood. For example, the Western Rivers and Great Lakes Rules give priority to vessels traveling downstream *(right)*. The other two codes make no distinction with regard to current direction. International and Great Lakes Rules demand five or more whistle blasts as a signal for danger, while Inland and Western Rivers Rules specify a minimum of four. Such differences are slight, but in moments of stress can be significant.

The best thing a neophyte skipper can do is to memorize those general Rules of the Road that apply to the waters he sails —particularly those having to do with hazardous channel navigation—so that they become second nature. In addition he will be wise to check the Coast Guard Pilot Rules for any special regulations or guidance; in a constricted channel there is no margin for error.

Under Western Rivers Rules, a boat coming downstream toward a bridge has right of way over an ascending boat—even if the latter is already under the bridge. The privileged craft, by sounding the danger signal, can force the other to back clear.

Coping with River Currents

Since Western Rivers Rules favor vessels moving with the current, the cruiser about to cross the starboard bow of the boat moving downstream immediately below must give way—although it would have the right of way in a normal crossing situation.

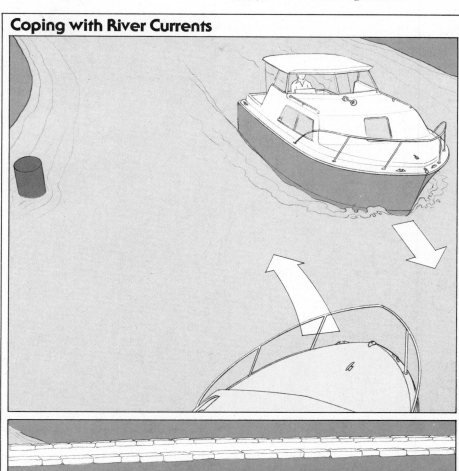

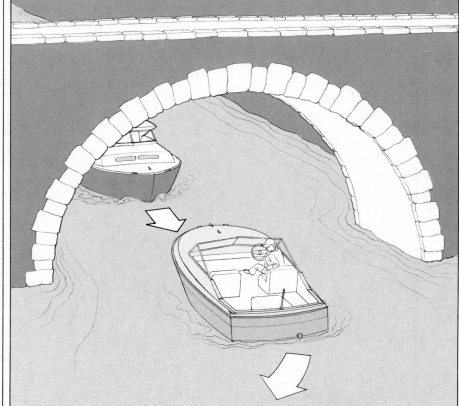

When a fog-bound boat runs aground,
International Rules require a special
signal: five seconds of rapid bell ringing,
preceded and followed by three separate and
distinct strokes of the bell at intervals of no
more than one minute. Inland Rules make no
provision for this situation, but good
seamanship dictates the use of this danger
signal as a warning to other boats.

A Guide to Fog Signals

Powerboats Underway	Inland: 1 four- to 6-second blast every minute. International: when moving, 1 blast every 2 minutes; when stopped, 2 blasts every 2 minutes. Great Lakes: 3 blasts a minute. Western Rivers: 2 short blasts followed by 1 long a minute.
Sailboats Underway	Inland, International and Great Lakes: starboard tack sounds 1 blast a minute; port tack, 2 a minute; wind abaft the beam, 3 a minute. Western Rivers Rules have no rules for sailboats.
Vessels at Anchor	Inland, International and Western Rivers: rapid ringing of a bell for 5 seconds every minute. International: ships over 350 feet sound a gong and a bell. Great Lakes: a bell every 2 minutes and blasts of 1 short, 2 long, 1 short every 3 minutes.
Towing Vessels	Inland and International: 1 prolonged blast plus 2 short per minute. Great Lakes: a steamer with a raft in tow sounds a whistle per minute. Otherwise the powerboat's underway signal is sounded. Western Rivers: 3 blasts per minute.
Vessels in Tow	Inland: same signal as towing boat. International: if manned, 1 prolonged blast plus 3 short. Great Lakes: 4 bells in groups of 2 every minute. No Western Rivers rule.
Vessels Aground	Inland: no special provision (see illustration above). International: anchor bell with 3 short strokes before and after the signal. Great Lakes: if in a channel, same as anchor signal. Western Rivers Rules: no provision.

Fog and Distress Signals

As the charts on these pages indicate, the four major sets of Rules of the Road do not, surprisingly, agree on very many details of their required fog and distress signals. However they are unanimous on a few basic principles. For example, all state that fog signals should be sounded in "fog, mist, falling snow or heavy rainstorms," and all caution boats in fog to proceed at "moderate" speed, which maritime courts have ruled can mean no forward motion whatsoever in very thick conditions. As an extra caution, International Rules stipulate that these procedures be followed even if a vessel has radar. Under Inland Rules, fog signals are given whenever visibility is reduced to one mile.

Although no Rules so state, a prudent seaman will sound fog signals before entering a fogbank, to alert any nearby vessels that might already be fogbound.

Fog signals are more than simple noises indicating a vessel's presence. When understood they provide other vital information, such as the size and limitation of maneuverability of a boat. They can even help to indicate a boat's specific activity, like which tack a sailboat is on.

In order to make proper fog or distress signals, powerboats must carry a whistle or, in Inland Waters, a siren. Sailboats must have a foghorn and both types of vessels are required to carry an efficient bell. Larger ships—over 350 feet long—must also have a gong or another instrument that is not easily confused with a bell, to alternate with the bell and warn other boats that a big ship is anchored.

Upside Down—and Out

One of the best-known visual distress signals in American waters is an inverted U.S. ensign. However, this signal is not recognized by the Rules, since other maritime nations have flags which appear the same whether right side up or upside down. The Coast Guard recommends arm-waving or other International signals—which are as visible and often quicker than capsizing the ensign.

How to Call for Help

The devices shown above are commonly used to signal distress. They are a ship's horn, a hand gun (often called a Very pistol) which fires brilliant flares into the air, and a hand-held smoke flare. These and other distress signals, recognized under the four Rules of the Road are listed below. But whether authorized or not, a good distress signal is any one that brings help.

Signals	Inland Rules	Great Lakes Rules	Western Rivers Rules	International Rules
A continuous sounding with any fog-signaling apparatus	day night	day night	day night	anytime
A gun or other explosive signal fired at intervals of about a minute	day night	day night	day night	anytime
Controlled flames on the vessel (as from a flare, burning tar barrel, etc.)	night	night	night	anytime
A signal consisting of a square flag having above or below it a ball or anything resembling a ball		day	day	anytime
A man standing in a conspicuous position, slowly and repeatedly raising and lowering his outstretched arms	day	day	day	anytime
Rockets or cartridges whose projectiles are red stars fired one at a time at short intervals		night	day night	anytime
The "N" and "C" flags of the International Code hoisted high in a ship's rigging			day	anytime
SOS: signal by radiotelegraphy or other signaling method consisting of the group ...———... in Morse Code				anytime
A radiotelephone signal consisting of the spoken word "Mayday"				anytime
A rocket parachute flare or a hand flare showing a red light				anytime
A smoke signal giving off a volume of orange-colored smoke				anytime

Lights on Inland Waters

The navigation lights of vessels at night convey an astonishing amount of information, and it is vital that the boatman master the meanings of these signals—known also as running lights. For the proliferation of pleasure craft and the attendant increased danger of collision make clear nighttime communication essential for survival.

The Rules of the Road carefully spell out the characteristics of each light: its position on the vessel, the required range of visibility, its color and the arc through which it must be visible *(below)*. Every sail or power craft is required to carry some combination of these lights that will identify it according to size and type. Some of the commonest regulations of the Inland Rules are shown on this page; the international versions are opposite.

The vessels in the drawings display only those lights that would be visible to a boatman observing the vessel from the viewpoint shown. In actual situations, the light patterns change as the vessel moves *(pages 118-119)*. By learning to read these patterns, a seaman knows in an instant on the darkest night which way a vessel is heading, how big it is and what it is doing. Most important, he knows immediately who has the right of way.

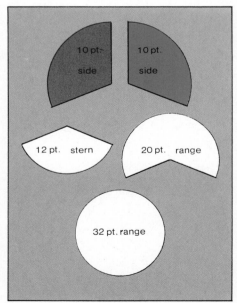

Each navigation light is of a specified color and must shine through a prescribed arc, measured in points, i.e., intervals of 11¼ degrees of a circle. Sidelights (top) are red to port and green to starboard and shine through 10 points—from dead ahead to two points abaft the beam. Stern lights are white 12-point lights; forward-shining range lights are white 20-point lights, and the all-round white range light shines through 32 points.

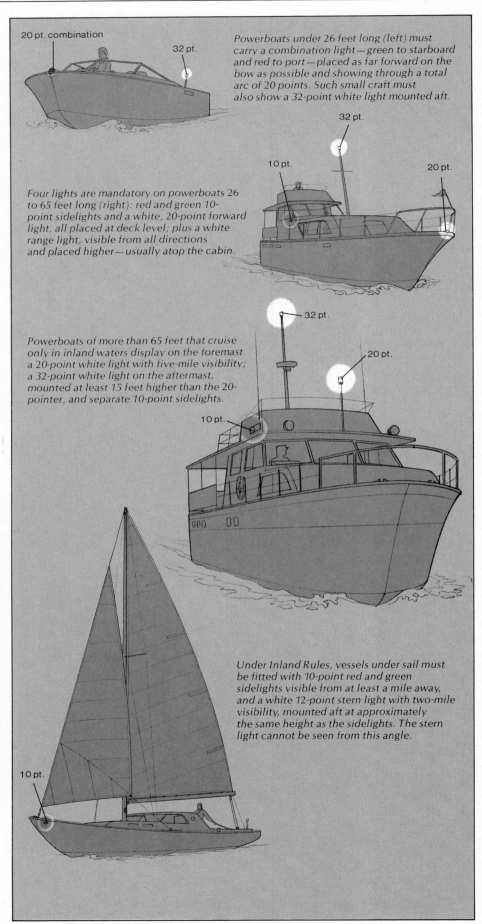

Powerboats under 26 feet long (left) must carry a combination light—green to starboard and red to port—placed as far forward on the bow as possible and showing through a total arc of 20 points. Such small craft must also show a 32-point white light mounted aft.

Four lights are mandatory on powerboats 26 to 65 feet long (right): red and green 10-point sidelights and a white, 20-point forward light, all placed at deck level; plus a white range light, visible from all directions and placed higher—usually atop the cabin.

Powerboats of more than 65 feet that cruise only in inland waters display on the foremast a 20-point white light with five-mile visibility; a 32-point white light on the aftermast, mounted at least 15 feet higher than the 20-pointer, and separate 10-point sidelights.

Under Inland Rules, vessels under sail must be fitted with 10-point red and green sidelights visible from at least a mile away, and a white 12-point stern light with two-mile visibility, mounted aft at approximately the same height as the sidelights. The stern light cannot be seen from this angle.

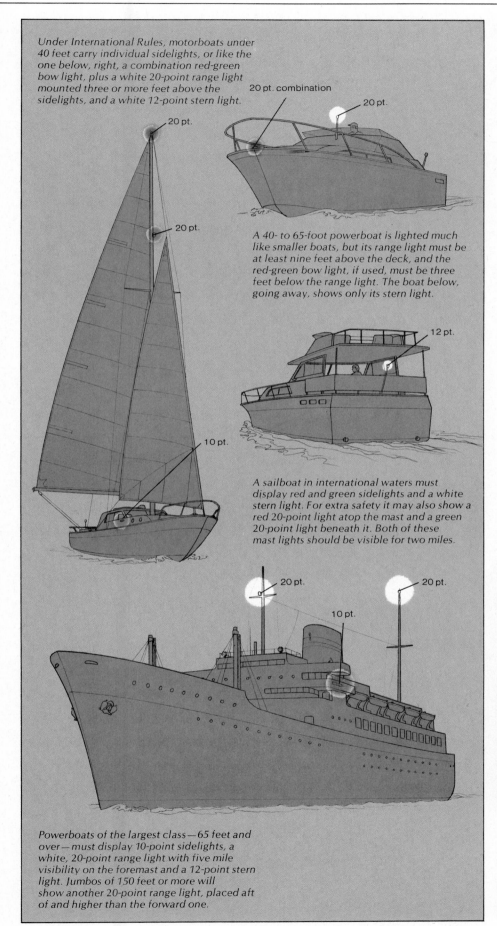

Under International Rules, motorboats under 40 feet carry individual sidelights, or like the one below, right, a combination red-green bow light, plus a white 20-point range light mounted three or more feet above the sidelights, and a white 12-point stern light.

20 pt. combination

20 pt.

20 pt.

20 pt.

A 40- to 65-foot powerboat is lighted much like smaller boats, but its range light must be at least nine feet above the deck, and the red-green bow light, if used, must be three feet below the range light. The boat below, going away, shows only its stern light.

12 pt.

10 pt.

A sailboat in international waters must display red and green sidelights and a white stern light. For extra safety it may also show a red 20-point light atop the mast and a green 20-point light beneath it. Both of these mast lights should be visible for two miles.

20 pt.

20 pt.

10 pt.

Powerboats of the largest class—65 feet and over—must display 10-point sidelights, a white, 20-point range light with five mile visibility on the foremast and a 12-point stern light. Jumbos of 150 feet or more will show another 20-point range light, placed aft of and higher than the forward one.

International Lights

On the high seas, running lights generally hang higher, are placed farther apart in a ship's rigging and shine more brightly so that they can be seen for much greater distances than the marine lights required by Inland Rules of the Road. The language the lights speak is clear and understandable to any seasoned seaman from Hoboken to Hong Kong—and for good reason: the International Rules were designed primarily to cover large vessels on long and often hazardous voyages, where mistakes can cost millions of dollars or hundreds of lives.

The lighting code in the International Rules takes precedence over all others. That is, when a boat sails from inland to international waters, it must be lighted according to International Rules, but vessels going the other way, into inland waters, need not display lights for Inland Rules. For years only oceangoing vessels and ferryboats were accorded this latter privilege. But in 1940, the Inland Rules were amended to permit all small yachts to maintain International Rules lights when sailing on inland waters.

The lighting regulations for International Rules were also amended in 1948, to accommodate small boats. For those small motorboats that cannot be fitted with lights to conform with the prescribed patterns, the international code now has less stringent rules plus an optional system of lights for a sailboat. These are explained in the illustrations on this page.

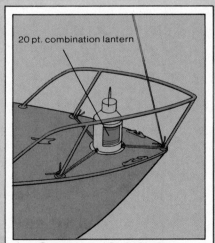

20 pt. combination lantern

An Option in Sidelights

The owner of a sailboat under 40 feet may, under International Rules, dispense with fixed sidelights and equip his boat instead with a half-red, half-green lantern to be fixed in the bow or at least kept ready for immediate use.

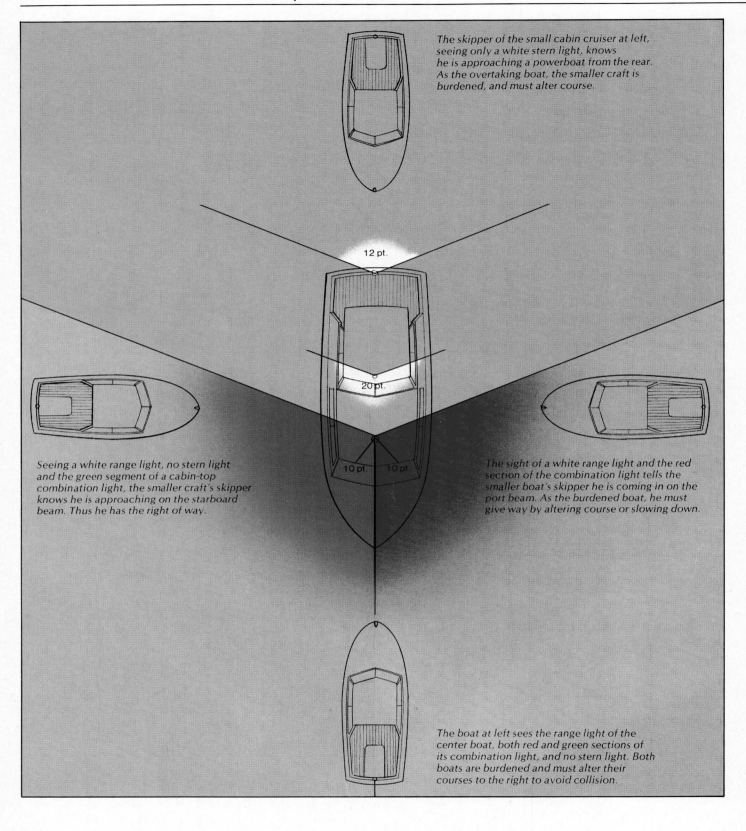

The skipper of the small cabin cruiser at left, seeing only a white stern light, knows he is approaching a powerboat from the rear. As the overtaking boat, the smaller craft is burdened, and must alter course.

12 pt.

20 pt.

10 pt.   10 pt.

Seeing a white range light, no stern light and the green segment of a cabin-top combination light, the smaller craft's skipper knows he is approaching on the starboard beam. Thus he has the right of way.

The sight of a white range light and the red section of the combination light tells the smaller boat's skipper he is coming in on the port beam. As the burdened boat, he must give way by altering course or slowing down.

The boat at left sees the range light of the center boat, both red and green sections of its combination light, and no stern light. Both boats are burdened and must alter their courses to the right to avoid collision.

Changing Look of Lights

The light patterns on the craft at right, lighted under International Rules, show it to be approaching. The vessel's green and red sidelights show simultaneously only when the vessel is viewed head-on. Similarly the white range lights on its masts appear in proximity only when seen from ahead.

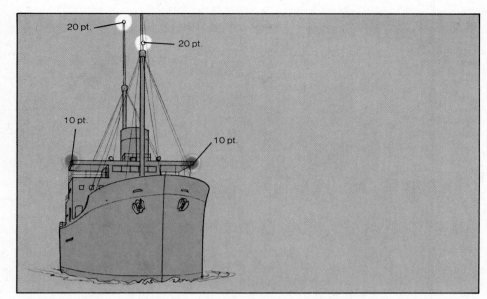

As the vessel turns, a stationary observer sees the range lights separate; the red (port) sidelight vanishes while the green (starboard) sidelight continues to show. This situation, together with the fact that her higher, after range light is on the left, indicates that the vessel is now moving from left to right.

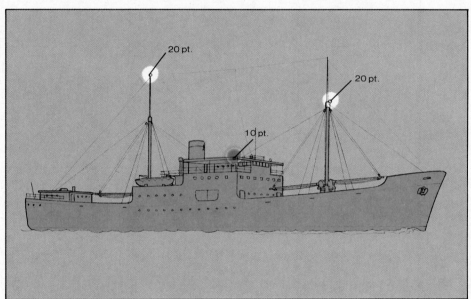

As the ship continues to turn, its 20-point range lights and its 10-point, starboard sidelight—all visible for only two points abaft the beam—vanish. The 12-point white stern light, visible only when the others cannot be seen, has appeared, a sure sign that the vessel is now heading away.

Inland Fishing and Towing

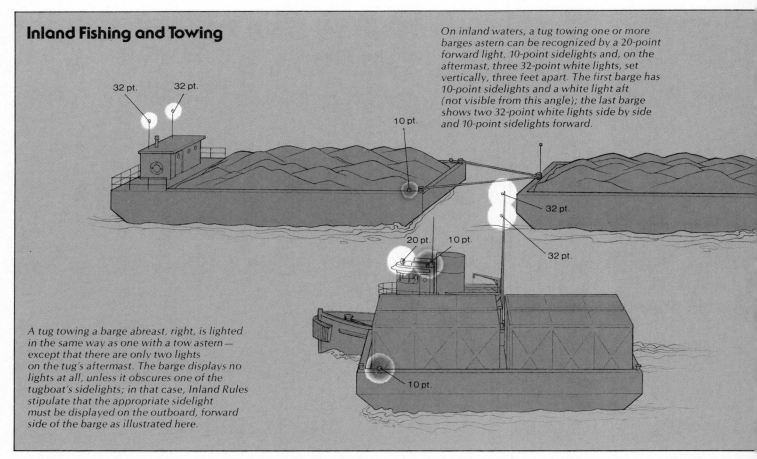

32 pt.   32 pt.

10 pt.

32 pt.

32 pt.

20 pt.   10 pt.

10 pt.

On inland waters, a tug towing one or more barges astern can be recognized by a 20-point forward light, 10-point sidelights and, on the aftermast, three 32-point white lights, set vertically, three feet apart. The first barge has 10-point sidelights and a white light aft (not visible from this angle); the last barge shows two 32-point white lights side by side and 10-point sidelights forward.

A tug towing a barge abreast, right, is lighted in the same way as one with a tow astern — except that there are only two lights on the tug's aftermast. The barge displays no lights at all, unless it obscures one of the tugboat's sidelights; in that case, Inland Rules stipulate that the appropriate sidelight must be displayed on the outboard, forward side of the barge as illustrated here.

Offshore Fishing and Towing

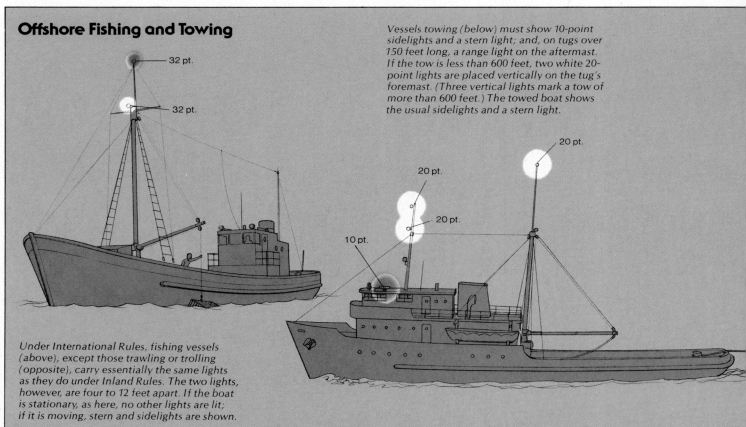

32 pt.

32 pt.

20 pt.

20 pt.

20 pt.

10 pt.

Vessels towing (below) must show 10-point sidelights and a stern light; and, on tugs over 150 feet long, a range light on the aftermast. If the tow is less than 600 feet, two white 20-point lights are placed vertically on the tug's foremast. (Three vertical lights mark a tow of more than 600 feet.) The towed boat shows the usual sidelights and a stern light.

Under International Rules, fishing vessels (above), except those trawling or trolling (opposite), carry essentially the same lights as they do under Inland Rules. The two lights, however, are four to 12 feet apart. If the boat is stationary, as here, no other lights are lit; if it is moving, stern and sidelights are shown.

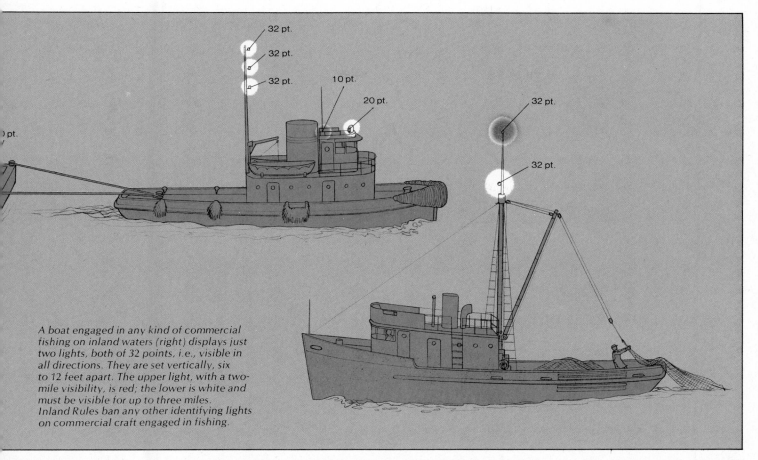

32 pt.

32 pt.

32 pt.

10 pt.

20 pt.

32 pt.

32 pt.

0 pt.

A boat engaged in any kind of commercial fishing on inland waters (right) displays just two lights, both of 32 points, i.e., visible in all directions. They are set vertically, six to 12 feet apart. The upper light, with a two-mile visibility, is red; the lower is white and must be visible for up to three miles. Inland Rules ban any other identifying lights on commercial craft engaged in fishing.

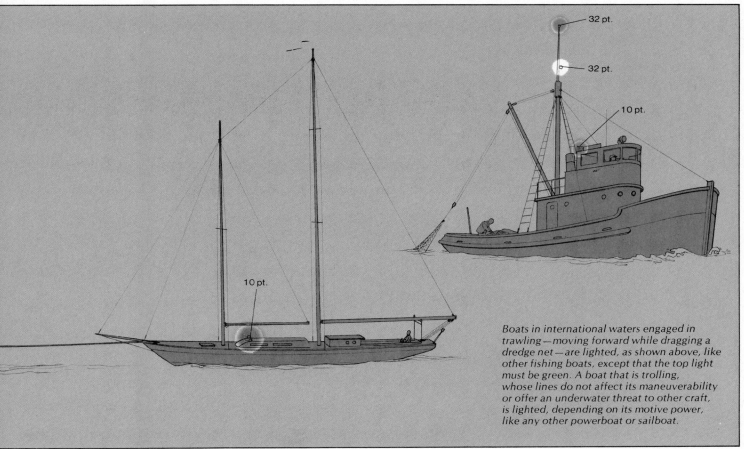

32 pt.

32 pt.

10 pt.

10 pt.

Boats in international waters engaged in trawling—moving forward while dragging a dredge net—are lighted, as shown above, like other fishing boats, except that the top light must be green. A boat that is trolling, whose lines do not affect its maneuverability or offer an underwater threat to other craft, is lighted, depending on its motive power, like any other powerboat or sailboat.

Lights for Anchoring and Distress

The International and Inland Rules require anchored vessels under 150 feet long to show a white light visible at night for two miles. A light of this type is shown below, properly displayed high in the forepart of both a small powerboat and a sailboat. Larger ships anchored at night display two white 32-point lights. The forward light must be at least 20 feet above the hull, and the aft, 15 feet below the forward.

Ships over 65 feet that are disabled—which nautical parlance describes as being "not under command," even if the commander is aboard—must display two red lights in a vertical line at least six feet apart (above, top), and stern and sidelights. These regulations occur in International and Great Lakes Rules and both sets of Rules also require a ship that has run aground to show the same red lights plus an anchor light. The Inland and Western Rivers codes make no mention of such emergency lights.

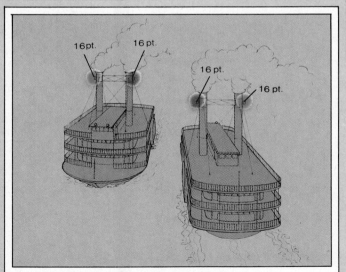

An Exception for Side-Wheelers

The Western Rivers Rules have a unique regulation governing the lights of "river steamers," a phrase which defines steam vessels with smokestacks set athwartships. The rule applies to survivors of the Mississippi River's fleet of old side-wheelers. As shown here, a red light on the port stack and a green light on the starboard stack bulge out like frog's eyes and shed 180-degree beams. Like no other side-lights afloat, each can be seen from both ahead and astern.

A Circus of Lights

A moored dredge with a scow alongside and a pipeline attached presents a spectacular display of special maritime lights. The dredge itself shows a white 32-point light at each corner, not less than six feet above the deck, and two red 32-point lights placed vertically no more than six feet apart and no less than 15 feet above the deck. The dredge also shows red 32-point lights to mark its mooring buoys. The scow has a six-foot-high white light at each outer corner. A series of amber lights, eight to 12 feet above the water, marks the pipeline.

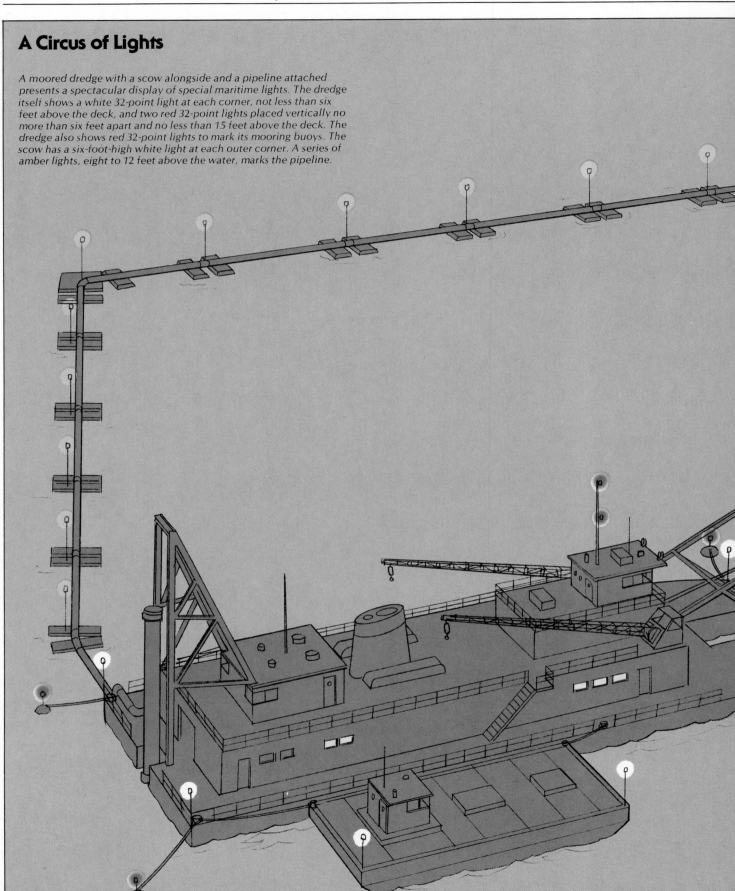

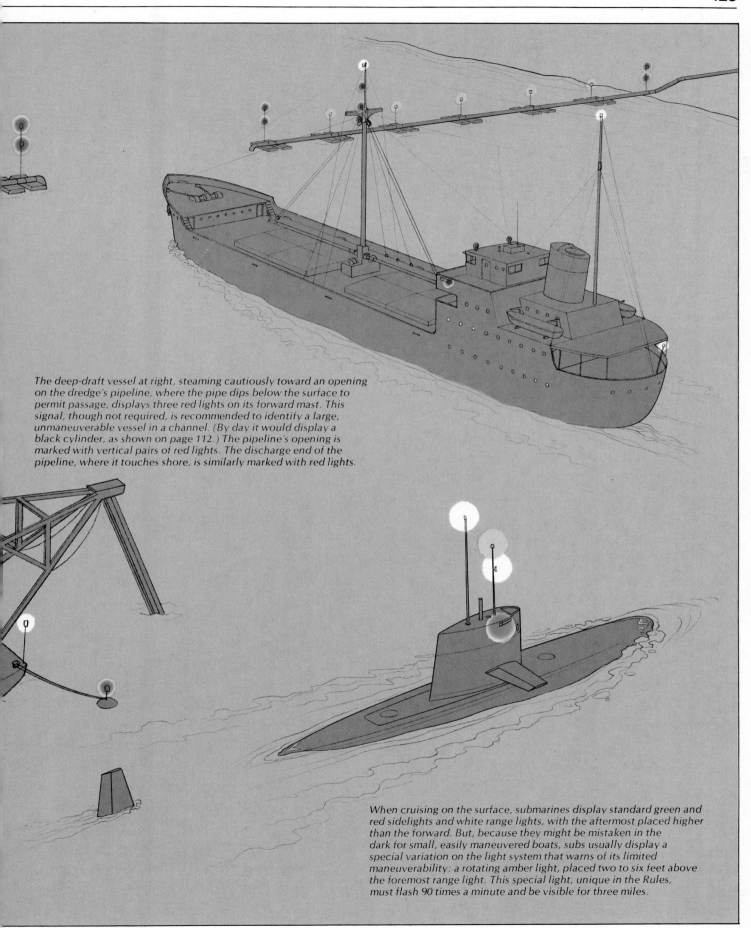

The deep-draft vessel at right, steaming cautiously toward an opening on the dredge's pipeline, where the pipe dips below the surface to permit passage, displays three red lights on its forward mast. This signal, though not required, is recommended to identify a large, unmaneuverable vessel in a channel. (By day it would display a black cylinder, as shown on page 112.) The pipeline's opening is marked with vertical pairs of red lights. The discharge end of the pipeline, where it touches shore, is similarly marked with red lights.

When cruising on the surface, submarines display standard green and red sidelights and white range lights, with the aftermost placed higher than the forward. But, because they might be mistaken in the dark for small, easily maneuvered boats, subs usually display a special variation on the light system that warns of its limited maneuverability: a rotating amber light, placed two to six feet above the foremost range light. This special light, unique in the Rules, must flash 90 times a minute and be visible for three miles.

5 A quarter of a century ago a boat on wheels was as rare a sight as a car afloat. But today, scenes like the one at left in the parking lot of a Los Angeles marina are repeated a thousandfold all across the United States. About one boatman in three now trailers his boat from home to water and back for every outing. Some vessels log more highway miles on a single vacation trip than they do nautical miles the rest of the year.

One major reason trailer boating has boomed so in popularity is the dramatic improvement of the equipment. In the early 1950s a trailer was little more than a crude platform on wheels. To launch his craft the boatman had

BOATS ON THE HIGHWAY

to back the trailer into the water until it (and sometimes his car's rear end) was sufficiently submerged to let the boat float free. Or he went to a launching site that had marine hoists capable of plucking the boat off the trailer and lowering it into the water.

Then in 1953 the first tilting trailer appeared—a modification designed to help a boatman launch and recover his vessel quickly, easily and without baptism by total immersion. In the next two decades the number of boat trailers soared: in 1950 fewer than 4,000 boat trailers were built; by 1973 an estimated 3.8 million were rolling. Thousands of new boat ramps were constructed; dozens of trailer designs evolved and trailering became a practicable and very economical way of life for the average boatman. A conventional boatyard today may charge the owner of a 20-foot boat hundreds of dollars each year for launching, mooring, hauling out and winter storage; but by spending just a part of that annual total to buy a trailer—that with proper maintenance will last him for many years—a boatman can do all these jobs himself. Furthermore, keeping the boat stored on a trailer out of the water much of the time can prolong hull life; and being able to tow the boat home makes maintenance an easy matter of spare-time tinkering.

In choosing a trailer the boatman should take special care to select one long and strong enough to carry his boat. Stamped on every trailer's frame is a maximum load capacity, expressed in pounds. No trailer should be loaded to more than about 85 per cent of this figure. Otherwise the trailer's tires, springs and frame may not stand up to the shock treatment of a bumpy road.

Every trailer must also have enough rubber rollers, or the padded supports called bunks, to cradle the hull adequately. For example, because so much of their weight bears on the keel, most deep-V and semi-V powerboat hulls—and all sailboats with retractable keels—need strong support all along the keel. If keel rollers are too widely spaced, the hull may warp. Any trailered boat with an outboard motor attached needs support directly under the transom; an engine-bearing transom that overhangs its supports may crack.

Along with these basics, the boatman must consider some other critical aspects of trailering. When buying a trailer he should ask a first-rate mechanic what kind of weight his car can safely tow. He should select a hitch with particular care, for the right kind of trailer hitch can make the difference between a contented car and a rambling wreck. A boatman also should think about whether to buy a manual or a power-driven winch, and he should be equally fussy in selecting the other vital accessories such as trailer brakes, lights, spare tire, dolly jack, side-view mirrors, boat tie-downs and engine or boat covers. He should review federal and state laws governing trailer use. Before hitting the highway, anyone new to trailering should get used to the maneuvering problems. An hour spent practicing backing, turning and parking in some open area—such as an empty parking lot—will enhance the boatman's skill in getting his craft to the water and home again.

This crowd scene at a Los Angeles marina indicates the diversity of boat trailers. The sailboat (with mast down) on a light trailer is flanked by powerboats on heavy-duty rigs.

The Basic Trailers

Almost all of the dozens of different kinds of trailers now available to boatmen are patterned on one of the three basic types shown here: a fixed-frame trailer, a tilt-bed model and a hybrid with fixed bed and pivoting roller arms. Each, in its way, includes the essentials for trailering and launching a boat: a wheeled platform, special supports for the hull, and equipment to help the boatman get his craft into the water and back out onto the trailer again with the least possible strain.

All have frames, usually built of steel tubes or girders, that are as strong and light as possible. From the frame rise wooden supports, padded to protect the boat's hull, or metal supporting arms fitted with tough rubber rollers to aid in sliding the boat off and into the water and back onto the trailer.

Trailers ride on one or more pairs of tires that are usually smaller than auto tires and are designed for higher pressures, which are marked on the tire along with load rating. Prudent trailer boatmen carry a spare trailer tire as well as a jack low enough to fit under the trailer, since many standard automobile jacks will not do the job. Single-axle trailers such as the three shown here generally can handle boats of up to 20 feet; larger and heavier craft may require trailers equipped with two or sometimes three axles as well as heavy-duty springs and brakes.

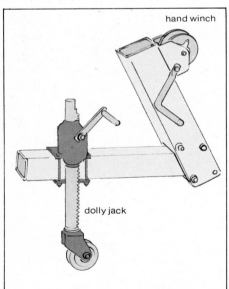

This detail of a trailer tongue shows two essential pieces of equipment. The winch, used for hauling a boat onto the trailer, is either hand-cranked as shown here or powered through a cable leading from the tow car's battery. The tongue wheel, or dolly jack, can be lowered for manhandling the trailer and cranked up for road trips.

Simplicity and economy are the virtues of the fixed-frame trailer, which has hull-cradling padded bunks at each side, and which often has rollers in the center to support the keel. Launching a boat from a fixed frame involves backing the trailer far enough into the water to let the boat float or be driven off. Though such a trailer costs less than a more complex model, its frame, bearings and lighting system need careful maintenance to offset the effects of frequent dunkings.

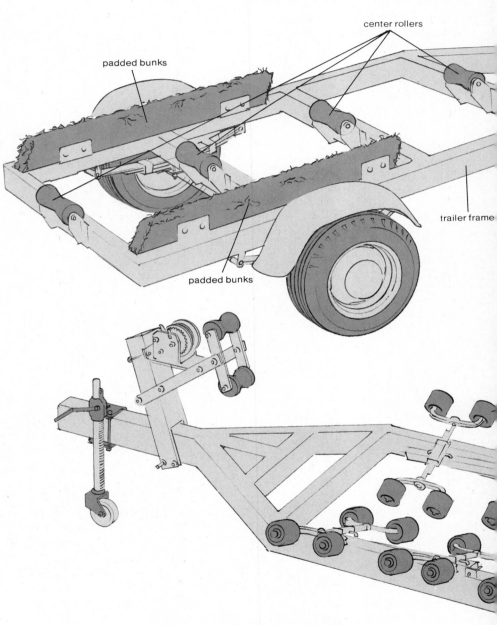

Ease in retrieving a boat from the water is the outstanding feature of the hybrid trailer, which combines a rigid frame with two or more sets of pivoting and roller-bearing supporting arms. This versatile design releases the boat into the water smoothly and its rollers support the hull at every step of the launch. On retrieval, the pivoting arms and rollers automatically guide the boat back onto the trailer in proper alignment.

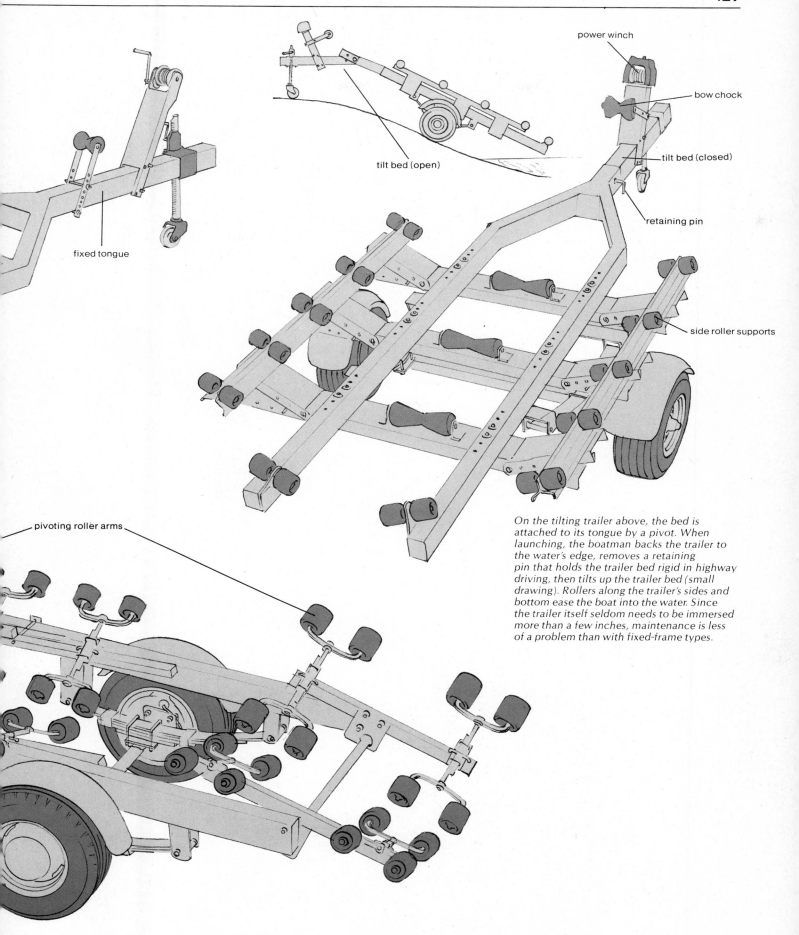

power winch

bow chock

tilt bed (closed)

retaining pin

fixed tongue

tilt bed (open)

side roller supports

pivoting roller arms

On the tilting trailer above, the bed is attached to its tongue by a pivot. When launching, the boatman backs the trailer to the water's edge, removes a retaining pin that holds the trailer bed rigid in highway driving, then tilts up the trailer bed (small drawing). Rollers along the trailer's sides and bottom ease the boat into the water. Since the trailer itself seldom needs to be immersed more than a few inches, maintenance is less of a problem than with fixed-frame types.

The first step in hooking up a trailer is to fit
the trailer coupler over the hitch ball; the
handle of the locking mechanism then moves
down (top arrow). Next, the plug from the
car's electrical system is connected to that of
the trailer's lighting system. Finally, the safety
chains are crossed over each other and
secured to the hitch platform to provide
a stable, direct pull if the hitch should part.

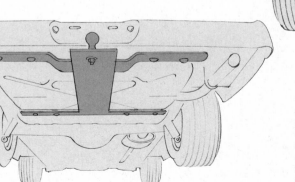

Two basic kinds of hitches take the
trailer's load in different ways. The crossbar
attachment is simply bolted to the car's
rearmost frame; this type will do for lighter
tongue weights—up to about 200 pounds.
Heavier loads may require an H-shaped
installation (left) that extends well forward
on the car's underbody in order to distribute
the trailer's load along the car's frame.

Hitches and Accessories

As with boat operation on the water, common sense as well as law determines the procedures and equipment that ensure safety in hauling a boat by trailer. Any trailer increases the demands on the car's power plant, and a prospective trailer purchaser should know how great a load his car can sustain. A reliable mechanic can tell whether a car will need new springs and shock absorbers, or alterations to its cooling system in order to bear the strain of hauling a trailer.

Fitting the car with the right hitch is equally important. A trailer not only pulls back horizontally against the hitch but also exerts a downward pressure—called tongue weight. Trailers behave best on the road when the tongue weight is between 5 and 10 per cent of the total weight; excessive tongue weight can depress the car's rear suspension so much that the front end lifts slightly and reduces steering control. A relatively simple hitch like the one in the upper part of the drawing at bottom left may work well with a gross weight of 2,000 pounds. A heavier load, however, will probably require a sturdier fixture like the one shown below it.

Every time the rig moves out, the parts of the hitch should be checked; and each step in hooking up must be done carefully to ensure a safe ride. No less crucial to safety are the various trailer accessories. Since a trailer-borne boat usually blocks at least part of the driver's normal rear view, extra rearview mirrors *(above, right)* are essential. The trailer also must have its own lights *(below, right)* connected to the car's electrical system.

Furthermore, most states require that a boat-bearing trailer weighing over 1,500 pounds must have brakes of its own—a practical precaution since a trailer that heavy adds about 40 per cent to the moving weight of a medium-sized car. Whenever the driver slows the car, this juggernaut surges against it, greatly increasing the strain on the car's brakes. If the trailer is the least bit out of line, the result can be a jackknife in which the car's rear end is shoved violently to one side while the trailer slews in the opposite direction.

All trailer brakes operate either as a response to pressure on the car's brake pedal or automatically, on their own. The latter type, called surge brakes, are controlled independently by a sensing device that is mounted in the coupler. When the car slows down, the sensor responds to any forward surge of the trailer by instantly activating the trailer's brakes.

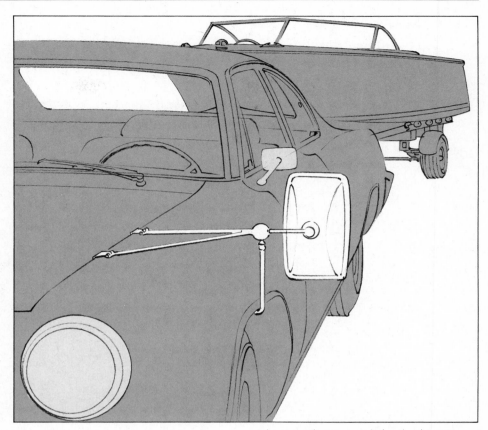

A large auxiliary mirror helps the driver to see around a boat trailer that otherwise would block the view of the road to the rear. Such towing mirrors can be temporarily mounted on a door or on a fender, as shown in the drawing above. They provide a rear view without blocking forward vision (many drivers fit one on each side) and can be removed when driving without trailer.

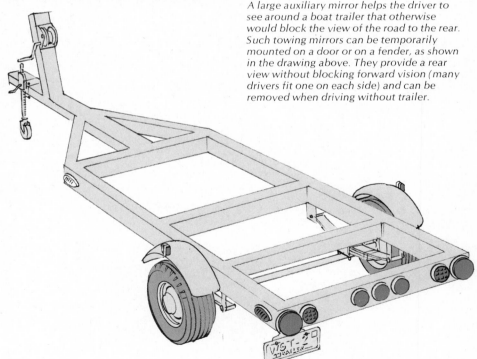

Federal lighting requirements for trailers include taillights (which also function as stop/turn signals), red and amber sidelight/reflectors, red rear reflectors and a license plate light. Trailers more than six feet eight inches wide must also have fender-mounted lights called clearance lights—amber forward and red to the rear—and three rear-end lights whose centers are six to eight inches apart.

How to Maneuver

Many boatmen find that handling a boat on the road can be almost as much of a challenge as maneuvering it on the water. Furthermore, successful trailering, like good boat handling, calls for practice and prudence. A car with a trailer in tow is longer and heavier than a car alone; it also burns more fuel, has less pickup and wears out its brakes faster. The driver therefore should avoid quick stops and sudden swerves. He should pass other cars only when necessary and allow extra time and space for passing.

It is also important to remember that a trailer is a long, heavy tail that can wag the car if not controlled. A trailer's higher-riding load makes it vulnerable to crosswinds or the drafts from passing trucks. Such a sidewise push may cause the best-designed of trailers to yaw—that is, to swing back and forth—especially if its weight is incorrectly distributed.

Fishtailing of this sort usually indicates insufficient weight on the hitch, a condition that can sometimes be corrected by stopping and shifting any heavy items in the boat farther forward, or by moving the boat up on the trailer. If all else fails, the trailer's axle can be repositioned farther back on the frame. But when the trailer starts acting up on the road, there is only one prudent immediate remedy: the driver must ease off on the car's throttle and slow down gently until the rig starts to behave itself.

At the beginning of the backing left turn illustrated above, the driver puts his hand at the bottom of the steering wheel and gives it a turn to the right (1). This maneuver jackknifes car and trailer until the boat's stern is pointed toward the head of the launching ramp. Then, with one hand again at the bottom of the steering wheel, the driver turns it counterclockwise (2). This second swing of the front wheels gets the car turning in the same arc as the trailer. If the driver has correctly calculated his approach angle, car and trailer will remain in the proper path as they move together onto the ramp. As the car and trailer fall into line on the ramp (3), the driver straightens his car's front wheels and eases the trailer down to the water's edge.

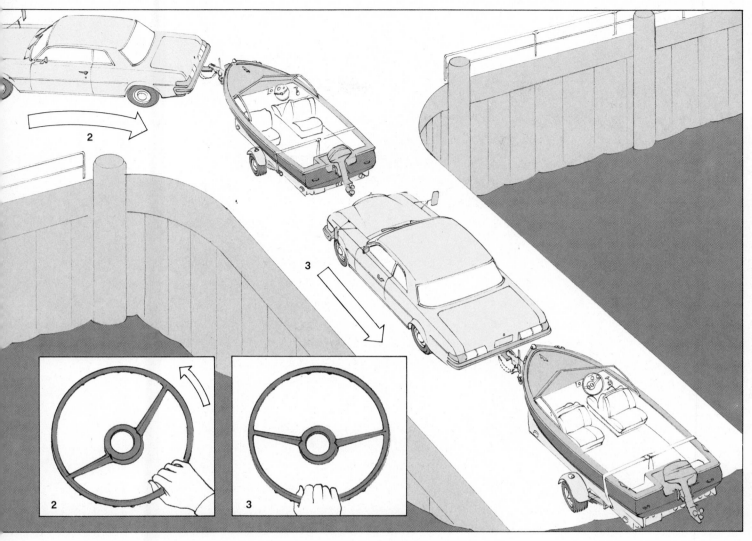

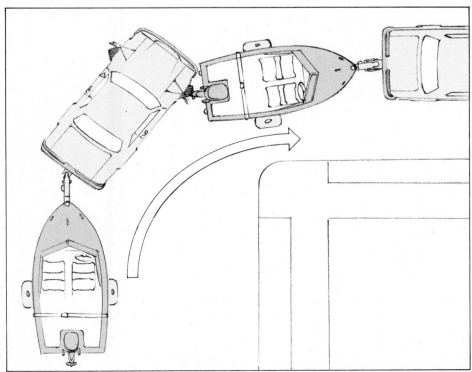

Going around a sharp corner with a trailer, the driver turns later than he would with a car alone. His rig is so long that at the apex of the turn the trailer will come closer to the curb than will the car. He must also move farther out from the curb before turning, a hazardous maneuver that obliges him to watch carefully for oncoming traffic.

Watching carefully, the driver eases his rig down the ramp, concentrating on keeping car and trailer aligned. In this demonstration the boat's tie-downs are still in place; on a busy day at the ramp, however, the boatman would have removed the tie-downs while the boat was still in the parking lot.

Steps for Launching

Launching a small boat from a trailer usually takes about 10 minutes, most of it spent getting the boat ready to hit the water. A smart boatman checks the ramp conditions, water depth, wind and current before approaching the ramp. If the water is low, for instance, the lower part of the ramp may be slippery, requiring extra caution in backing down.

In a busy launching area with rigs lined up for turns at the ramp, it is wise and courteous to make preparations in the parking lot to reduce time spent on the ramp. The crew removes the boat cover, secures the drain plug, makes fast the bow and stern lines and fenders, and removes the engine brace—a bar that locks the engine in place and keeps it from jouncing when the rig is on the road.

Then the driver maneuvers his trailer to the top of the ramp, with a crew member standing by to guide him down. The sequential launching steps that follow are illustrated here and on the next two pages. The trailer in the photographs is a tilt-frame model; with a fixed-frame rig, the skipper would back the trailer far enough into the water to float the boat off.

While parked, the skipper also removes the last of the boat's tie-downs. The boat is now secured to the trailer only by a line from winch to bow, but it is heavy enough to stay put until tilted into the launch position.

Stopping halfway down the ramp, the skipper removes the pin that locks the tilt frame in place for towing. Enough of the boat's weight rests forward of the tilting axis to keep the frame from rocking up prematurely.

Backing down the last few feet, the driver
watches his spotter, who signals when there
is enough water under the boat's stern for
a launch. Under ideal conditions, this occurs
when only about the lower third of the
trailer's tires are wet (below, left).
The outboard motor has been tilted up out of
harm's way, the transom drain plug is in place
and the boat is ready to go into the water.

Immersion of a trailer's wheels even this far
can adversely affect the brakes and wheel
bearings, especially in salt water. But if the
ramp has a shallow pitch, sometimes it is
necessary to wet the wheels completely in
order to get to deep enough water to launch
the boat. In that case the careful skipper
applies his dampened brakes cautiously en
route home—and later hoses down the parts
of the trailer that got wet at launching.

Just before the final moment, the skipper chocks his car's rear wheels. He has already set the emergency brake and put the car in gear; chocking relieves some of the strain on brake and transmission and will doubly ensure that he does not launch his car along with his boat. Here the chock is a brick, but a rock or chunk of wood will do.

With the bow line attached to a cleat and held by a crew member, the boatman now disconnects the winch line from the eye in the boat's stem. After the launch, the crew member will guide the boat away from the ramp. In a crowded harbor or in a strong wind or current, he might also have to use a stern line to control the craft.

Putting his back into it, the skipper tilts up the trailer's bed and his 1,200-pound boat along with it. To upend a heavier boat he might need the assistance of a crew member to help start the boat sliding.

With the outboard's stern in the water, the boatman stands dryshod on shore; the boat's momentum carries it the rest of the way off the trailer. Were he alone, he would have had to handle the bow line himself.

Hauling Out

Hauling a boat out of the water and back onto a trailer is basically a reversal of the launching technique. Hauling out begins with backing the trailer down the ramp again and chocking the car's wheels. With bow and stern lines, boatman and crew guide the boat up to the trailer. Then, for the first and only time in the launch-retrieval cycle, the boatman himself has to go into the water.

While a crew member with a stern line keeps the boat from drifting, the skipper wades out and attaches the winch line to the eye in the bow of the boat. He carefully aligns the boat with the bed of the trailer; if the boat slips out of alignment during loading, the skipper will have to push it off the trailer and start the whole job over again.

Making sure that the outboard motor is tilted up out of the way of any underwater obstructions, the boatman then winches the boat back up onto the trailer. He pauses occasionally to see that boat and trailer are still aligned. As the boat moves forward, its weight settles the tilting bed back down to the horizontal and the boatman locks the trailer assembly in place.

Once he has driven the trailer up and off the ramp, the skipper shifts cargo from boat to car, secures tie-downs and boat or engine covers, and installs the engine brace. Before moving out of the parking area, he also double-checks the hitch, sees to it that the safety chains are fastened and makes sure that the trailer's brakes and all of its lights are working properly. The boat and trailer are then ready to go back on the road.

While his crew tows the boat into retrieving position with bow and stern lines, the skipper pulls the winch line out to the rear of the trailer. The power winch (foreground) mounted on the trailer's tongue is connected to the car's battery by the cable at the lower right-hand corner of the photograph. The smaller line across the top of the winch provides remote control of the winch motor.

A closer look at the winch shows the spring-loaded power switch attached to the remote-control line by an S-shaped hook. A pull on the line moves the switch and starts the winch motor; slacking the line will shut it off.

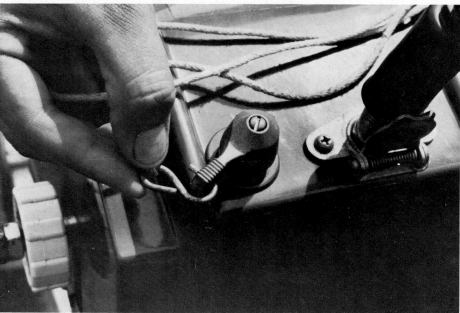

Protected by hip-high wading boots, the skipper attaches his winch line to the bow of the craft and pulls the bow up to the rear end of the trailer. A crew member, out of view at the right, continues to tend a stern line to keep the boat from drifting out of alignment with the trailer. As the boat swings into position, the skipper starts the remote-controlled winch and the boat begins inching onto the trailer.

Holding the winch control line with one hand and steadying the bow with the other, the skipper peers beneath the boat to make sure it is still aligned with the support system of the trailer's tilted bed. Meanwhile the crew tends the stern line until the boat is safely aboard the trailer. If the skipper were alone, he would have to tend the line himself.

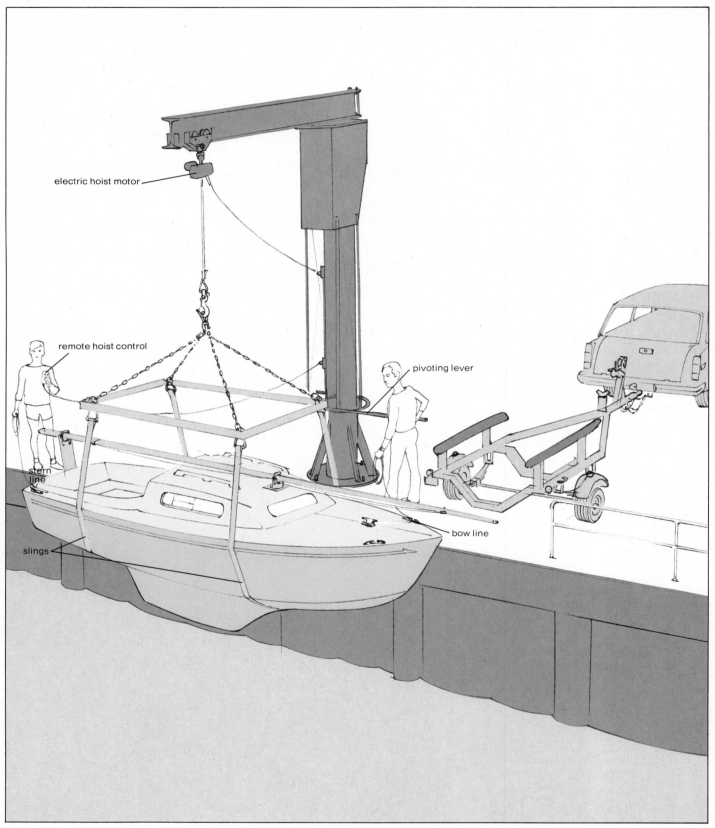

electric hoist motor

remote hoist control

pivoting lever

stern line

slings

bow line

This marine hoist, turned by a pivoting lever, swivels in an arc that allows the boatman to fix a pair of slings around his craft while it sits on the trailer, then pluck the boat up and lower it into the water. The skipper shown here is controlling the hoist with a remote switch while also tending the stern line; a crewman holds a bow line to keep the boat from banging against the pier. When the boat is launched, the skipper and his crew will remove the slings and step the mast.

Trailers for Sailors

The increasing popularity of trailer-borne sailing has stimulated the development of rigs designed, like the ones on this page, to carry sailboats with centerboards or retractable keels *(right),* or fixed keels *(below).* Sailboats with hulls too deep and complex to fit handily on tilting-bed trailers must be launched by submerging the trailer until the boat floats off. This approach requires either equipping the trailer with a telescoping tongue, or—with lightweight boats—unhooking the trailer at the water's edge and trundling it by hand out into deeper water.

An alternative and equally effective method of launching is the marine hoist *(left)* used for both sailboats and powerboats at many public facilities. Yacht clubs also frequently use hoists to launch visiting trailer-borne sailboats, or resident boats that might otherwise take up scarce mooring or dock space.

Although a powerboat, once launched, is ready to go, the skipper who has trailered his sailboat to water still has to step the mast and bend on the sails. Such extra effort, however, is a small price willingly paid by thousands of sailors who now trailer their boats to remote mountain lakes or trek across deserts *(overleaf)* to launch their craft in waters they could never have reached before.

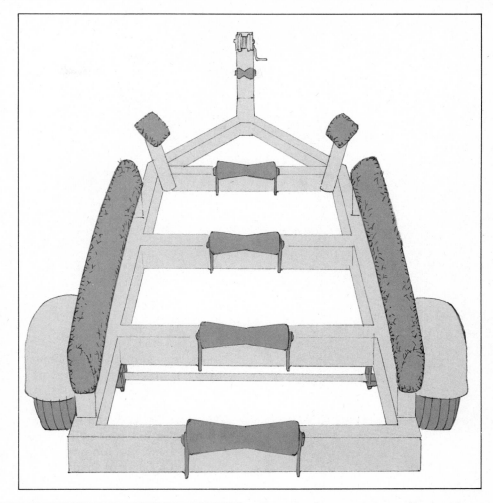

The trailer above, made for a sailboat with a full underbody but no fixed keel, has raised, padded bunks to hold the topsides securely. Rollers down the center of the bed bear much of the hull's weight—and also serve to ease the boat on and off. Although this trailer is a typical fixed-bed model, some small sailboat trailers are made with tilting beds, like the tilt-frame rig on page 129.

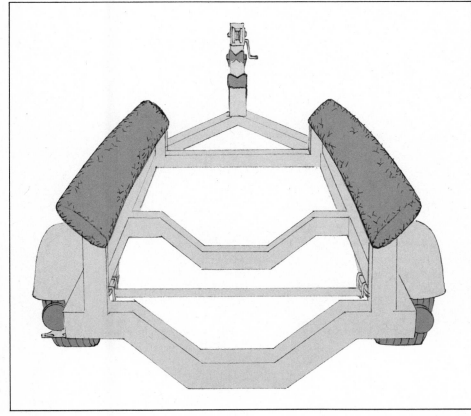

The trailer at left is designed for a boat with a deep fixed keel. Like other sailboat trailers, it has raised bunks for hull support. Instead of having rollers along the bottom, however, it has U-shaped cross braces designed to accommodate the keel. Most such trailers are custom-made for a specific class of sailboat.

A caravan of sailors on wheels crosses Mexico's Sonora Desert on the way to an Easter week regatta in the Gulf of California. All these boatmen, some of them from as far away as Minnesota, are members of the North American Sailing Association, which is one of several organizations of trailer sailors. Their boats, ranging from 20 to 26 feet in length, were designed specifically for trailer sailing.

6 It will not take a tyro skipper long to discover that there is a lot more to handling a boat than hoisting sail or starting engines, abiding by the Rules of the Road, or making skillful landings on his return to port. He will inevitably encounter situations, both predictable and unexpected, to which he must apply special techniques and seasoned judgment. Some of these out-of-the-ordinary circumstances that a boatman is likely to meet—and what to do in each instance—are described on the following pages. For each of these predicaments, and most others as well, there will be one or more workable solutions—and at least one disastrous approach. By making sure in advance

COMMON SENSE IN TIGHT PLACES

that his boat is equipped to handle the ordinary run of emergencies and by combining common sense with a few basic principles, any boatman can feel reasonably confident of making the right choices.

The skipper in the scene at left, for example, is successfully running a choppy inlet by applying the principles explained on pages 158-159. If the seas racing through this bottleneck were any rougher, he might, by the application of common sense, decide to wait for the calmer waters of flood tide before making his run. Some situations are easier to anticipate than others. A boatman who plans a trip that includes canal locks can easily prepare himself and his boat for the special problems of locking. If a small-boat sailor is required to steer one of a string of dinghies being towed in tandem to the start of a race, he finds out what will be expected of him and plans accordingly. If he intends to traverse heavily trafficked waters, he makes sure he knows how to deal with large and potentially dangerous wakes.

But even the most well-prepared skipper cannot predict exactly when or where he will run his boat aground, or when he will find himself—or a fellow mariner—in need of a tow. Sooner or later anyone who does any amount of boating will wind up facing one or another of these common emergencies. The careful skipper expects the unexpected, and he keeps on hand the basic tools needed to attack nearly any problem likely to come his way. To bail out a swamped boat he carries a bilge pump and a bucket. If he is navigating in shallow waters where grounding seems a strong possibility, he makes sure he has a small anchor with which to kedge himself off a shoal. And since a great many situations involve a need for lines and fenders, he always keeps two or three fenders on board as well as a few extra lines in the rope locker, along with the beer.

His most important tool, however, is the common sense that will help him to identify a change in conditions before it becomes an emergency and to deal with emergencies before they turn into disasters. Common sense will not only tell him what to do in most of the situations he will encounter but will also, and often more important, tell him what not to do.

Good timing contributes greatly to the success of any maneuver. The skipper who picks the right moment to follow a wave through an inlet will come through safe and dry. The boatman who waits for a big wake to die down a bit before crossing it will improve his chances of successfully applying his wake-crossing techniques. A mariner eager to help the struggling crew of a capsized sailboat will find his intervention both more welcome and more helpful if it begins with a cautious reconnaissance and continues with a careful check at each step to ensure all hands are safe and accounted for.

Few nautical problems will fail to yield to the boatman who approaches them with care and confidence, armed with a specific knowledge of how his boat responds in any given situation—and armed also with common sense and enough rope.

In the middle of a dangerous inlet off the coast of New Jersey, the skipper of a small outboard carefully times his progress in order to keep safely ahead of the following wave.

In the top picture above, a powerboat skipper
prepares a towline by making up a bridle, a
separate piece of line secured to the two
stern cleats of his boat. Then he ties one end
of his nylon towline to the bridle with a
bowline or other knot that will slide along
the bridle without binding. Finally he ties two
buoyant seat cushions to the other end of
the towline to serve as an improvised float.

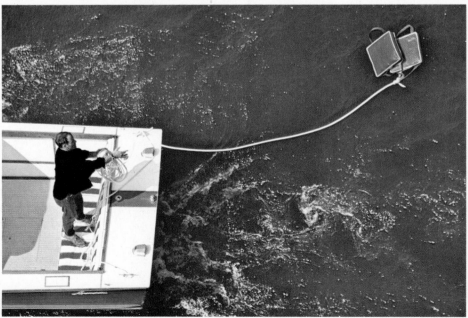

The rescuer tosses the cushions with towline
attached out over the stern of his boat,
heaving them far enough to avoid entangling
his propeller. Then he pays out enough line
to tow them within range of the sailboat.

Trailing his towline, the powerboat skipper
approaches the disabled sailboat from
the leeward side, circling around to his left
so as to drag the buoyed towline across
the sailboat's bow. A crewman in the towboat
tends the towline, while on the sailboat
one of the crew kneels in the bow
with a boathook, waiting to fish out
the towline when it gets close enough.

Picking up a Cripple

Almost every boatman at some time in his career afloat will find himself cast either as the victim of a disabling mishap or as the rescuer. The illustrations on these and the next two pages demonstrate basic steps that he should know to act either part successfully.

The disabled craft in the rescue operation shown here is a 26-foot cruising sailboat whose headstay has let go, weakening the mast's support so that sails cannot be hoisted. The powerboat, a single-screw inboard, is also 26 feet long—but it could easily be smaller, since under favorable conditions a small boat can tow a vessel more than twice its size.

Before setting up the tow, the skipper of the rescuing boat must find out what is wrong. To try to tow a boat that is leaking badly and likely to sink, for instance, might well do more harm than good. In such a case the prudent course might be to take the crew off the crippled vessel and call the Coast Guard.

If a tow does seem safe, the prospective rescuer usually passes a line to the disabled craft. Obviously the line should be strong enough for the job; nylon is the best material since it has great strength as well as considerable elasticity. The elasticity absorbs the shock of towing and reduces the strain of sudden jerks against chocks and cleats. A long towline is better than a short one; added length means added give in the line. The bigger the tow and the rougher the water, the longer the line should be.

In calm weather the rescuer can come alongside the disabled boat and hand a line across. But in rough conditions, when approaching close enough to heave a line would be hazardous, the rescuer should stand off and float a line down to the tow, as shown on these pages. The crew of the tow takes the line aboard and makes it fast to the strongest fixture possible (overleaf). Then the towing operation can begin—and the best advice for the skipper of a towboat on how to proceed is summed up in one word: slowly.

A sailor on the disabled boat plucks the towline from the water by reaching with his boathook under the line and pulling up to hook it. After he has untied the cushions, he will then secure the line to his own boat.

For many sailboats, the best place to fasten the towline is the base of the mast—and a bowline is the best knot to tie it with (below). The mast is stronger than any cleat; it is on the centerline so that the towed vessel is less likely to yaw while underway; and it is easily accessible if a sudden emergency should arise requiring that the line be cut.

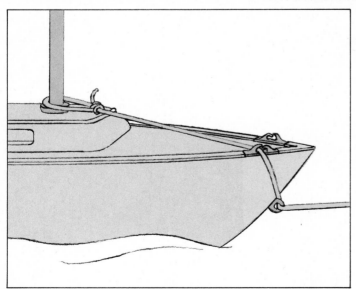

A light boat often can be towed by the bow eye, installed on many boats for use in trailering; but on a heavy boat (above) the mast should take the strain. The line goes through the bow eye—to keep it centered— then through a bow chock to the mast.

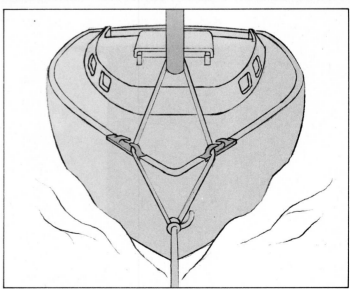

Many skippers prefer to pass the towline through one bow chock, around the mast, back through the other bow chock and then tie it off out in front of the bow. The mast absorbs the strain of the tow, while the two chocks keep the towline well centered.

With the towline passed through the bow eye and a bow chock and secured to the mast, the sailboat is ready to be towed. The powerboat begins a wide turn, moving off very slowly in order to bring the line gradually taut without jerking it. On the sailboat the helmsman prepares to follow the powerboat's turn before straightening out astern of it.

No matter what direction the towline pulls, the bridle on which it slides divides the strain between the towboat's two stern cleats.

Homeward bound, the towing boat moves at a slow, steady pace while the helmsman being towed follows the other's course as closely as possible. The towline is tended by the sailboat's crew, who should keep the distance between boats as great as possible while they are in open water. Once in a crowded harbor, however, the line will have to be shortened for close maneuvering.

Aid for an Upset

A powerboat skipper who spots an overturned craft like the sailing dinghy at right should always investigate to see if he can help. Often, the sailboat's crew will be able to cope alone; but sometimes, even if they seem to be righting the boat, heavy winds or waves may make it impossible for the sailors to keep it upright long enough to bail it out. Sails and rigging may be damaged or tangled beyond the crew's ability to get the craft moving again.

Whatever the circumstances, the seagoing samaritan should approach the situation cautiously. In any rescue operation, and especially one involving people in the water, an enthusiastic but careless rescuer can do more harm than good. He should first hail those in the water to make sure they want his help; if so, he should slowly nose up to the capsized craft from downwind. As soon as he is at the scene, he should shut off his engine; not only is a turning propeller a menace to people in the water, but it can easily be fouled and immobilized by the various lines—sheets, halyards or painter—that are bound to be trailing in the water from the overturned sailboat. Using the rescue boat as a platform, all hands can concentrate on getting the capsized vessel upright, bailed out and ready to resume operations.

In many cases, however, a craft so stricken may be in no condition to continue sailing, or its sodden crew members may be in bad shape themselves. In such circumstances, the rescuer should stand ready to supply one final good turn—a tow back to port.

Approaching a capsized sailing dinghy, the skipper of a small outboard (above) comes close enough to size up the situation and to ask the victims of the upset if he can be of any help. Given an affirmative answer, he takes a gingerly course to leeward so that he can make an upwind approach and avoid being blown into the dinghy or the men clinging to it. When he is a few yards downwind of the victims, the skipper should cut his engine and coast up alongside.

Using the powerboat as a platform, the three men right the dinghy (below), whose rigging has become so snarled that the sail cannot be lowered. The rescuer uses his bilge pump to help bail the water-filled craft while one sailor holds the dinghy alongside. The other sailor, still in the water, steadies the dinghy with one hand and bails with the other.

Since the dinghy can't be sailed home, the rescuer sets out to tow it with a line from the dinghy's bow eye made fast to the powerboat's stern cleat. The tangled mainsail has been detached from the boom so it will not fill with wind. One sailor rides in the towboat, watching the towline; the other stays aboard the dinghy to steer, keeping his weight well aft to prevent the bow from digging into the water and slewing the craft.

The alongside tow shown here begins at top left. A 25-foot inboard-outboard, which is securely tied to its tow, a disabled 37-foot cabin cruiser, backs away from the dock. The towboat's skipper uses his engines both as motive power and for steering: with bursts of forward and reverse he swings the tow around (center), then backs again to swing both sterns to port (bottom). As direction changes, the towing strain alternates from one set of lines to the other. The turn completed, the skipper puts both engines into forward and moves out (above). On the disabled boat a bow lookout watches for obstructions.

Towing Alongside

Sometimes a boat needs a tow in close quarters where more control is required than the usual towing method permits. One solution, shown on these two pages, is called alongside towing; it is used in this case to pull a disabled cabin cruiser away from a pier, turn it in a narrow slipway and push it out to a mooring in the harbor. Though recommended for use only in calm waters, this technique is an easy and efficient way for a small boat to maneuver a much larger one by pushing, pulling, turning and nudging.

The key to the maneuver is the arrangement of lines used to secure the two boats so tightly that, no matter what direction the boats turn in, they move as one. As shown in the diagram at left below, two lines take the strain of forward and reverse towing, while bow and stern lines help to keep the vessels properly positioned. All run diagonally from one boat to the other; the reverse towline and stern line act together when the towboat is reversing; the forward towline and bow line come into play when it is going forward.

Nearly as important as the lines are the fenders, which make it possible to hold the boats close together without damaging their topsides. The word fender (a shortening of defender) covers a variety of buffers used to keep a boat from banging into or rubbing against another object to the detriment of paint and hull. The air-filled plastic fenders used in this case are specifically made for the job; but many fenders are improvised from old rope, and in a pinch almost anything—buoyant cushions, old automobile tires, even bundles of old clothing—will do.

In alongside towing, two towlines are tied to a stern cleat in the towed boat; one to the towboat's stern, the other to its bow. These do the work, while bow and stern lines keep the towed boat from swinging away. Fenders hang from the boat with the higher freeboard.

The helmsman of the small outboard motorboat above is demonstrating impeccable technique in crossing the wake of a large powerboat. He has throttled down his engine, waited for the larger vessel to move ahead to a safe distance and is crossing the wake perpendicularly. He can now speed up and resume his former course.

The skipper at right is taking his boat across the heavy crest of a wake too soon and too fast. Passing close astern of the vessel making the wake, he encounters the highest part of the wave. And going at high speed increases the chance that the wheel will be jarred from his hands; uncontrolled, his boat could flip over or throw him out in an instant.

Crossing a Wake

The mere sight of the churning wake of a large vessel seems to bring out the daredevil in many small-boat skippers. Large boats, like high-speed ferries, which drag steep wakes behind them, often attract a flotilla of small pleasure craft like those shown below, whose owners enjoy darting in and out of the rolling wakes like frolicking water bugs. Indeed, there is no doubt that surfing a small boat on a large wake is the kind of thrilling, roller coaster sport that many incautious boatmen seem to find irresistible.

There is also no doubt that for all but the expert boatman this is a dangerous game. In fact, banging through cresting wakes is one of the most frequent causes of small-boat accidents. Improperly approached, the steep, often cresting waves of a heavy wake can jar a boat out of control or flip it over like a playing card.

It is impossible to avoid wakes altogether, however, and a good seaman learns that there is a correct way to cross them, as shown in the large picture at left. It usually involves cutting down speed, falling back and changing course to attack the wave at a perpendicular angle. After crossing the wake, he can increase speed and continue on course. This may seem tedious to a boatman in a hurry, but it is the only really safe way to approach a heavy wake.

Occasionally, however, wakes can be a powerboatman's friend. Particularly in rough seas, the broad track streaming out directly behind a large vessel may be the smoothest water around. A boatman can avoid a good deal of rough and wet riding by following along at a respectful distance from the larger craft, convoyed between the trailing waves on either side. But he should be careful to keep that distance, to stay clear of the dangerous turbulence often thrown up by a big ship's props.

The boatman at left playing games in the trough of a vessel's tumbling wake risks the dangers of surfing down the face of a wave and ramming his bow into the next one or of slewing around and broaching. If he wants to overtake the bigger boat, his safest procedure is to move out to one side and keep beyond the wake's wave pattern.

Crew members of a grounded 43-foot sloop
get ready to free the boat by kedging, having
first dropped the sails. Here they put in the
dinghy a small Danforth-type anchor (known
as a lunch hook because it is too light for
permanent anchoring). The regular anchor
rode is shackled to the working anchor,
so they use a heavy spinnaker sheet instead.

A crew member rows the kedge to deep
water, taking it in the direction he wants the
sloop to follow when strain is put on the
kedge line. If the water were rough and the
anchor heavier and hard to handle, he might
have hung the hook in the water over
the dinghy's transom on a short line; then he
could drop the anchor simply by untying it.

Resorting to acrobatics, the crew members concentrate their weight on the end of the boom in order to heel the boat slightly to port. This serves two purposes: it helps loosen the grip of mud or sand on the keel, and by canting the keel an inch or two, might raise it from the bottom enough to free it. The skipper, meanwhile, sets the kedge anchor by jerking hard on the line; next he will take the line forward to the boat's biggest winch in order to gain maximum hauling power to pull the boat back off the mud into deeper water.

Getting Unstuck

Going aground is a mishap that most boatmen have to cope with eventually—especially if they own a deep-draft sailboat like the sloop at left. Sometimes this can be serious. A pounding surf can smash to pieces a vessel stuck on a rocky shore; or a boat may be grounded so hard that only a tug can get her off. But such disasters fortunately are rare.

More often a skipper has merely cut a sandy point too fine, or edged in too close to the shore. The signs are sadly unmistakable. First there is a crunch of the keel grating on gravel or plowing through mud or sand; then a bump or two and suddenly forward motion stops. But the right techniques and a little luck will usually have the craft on her way.

The first thing a skipper must do is make sure he does not get stuck harder. If he is under power, he should immediately go into neutral; if he is sailing, he should lower his sails. His next concern—after making sure no one has fallen overboard in the excitement—should be for the boat's hull. A boat that has been holed at or below the waterline should be left aground until repairs are made and the water pumped out. The ground may be all that is keeping the boat from sinking.

If there is no serious damage, a powerboat skipper will usually try to back his craft off. But he should first make sure the propeller and rudder are undamaged; if so, a crewman may still have to go over the side and clear away obstructions so that the boat can safely back out.

The crew of any boat stuck in sand or mud may be able to work it loose by rocking the boat from side to side to break the suction of the mud on the keel—a tactic known in the days of sail as sallying ship. Heeling the boat to one side, either by hoisting sail again or by using crew weight *(left)*, often helps as well by reducing the keel's draft. But usually, if the motor will not do the job, the best bet is to row or carry an anchor out to deep water *(far left)* and try to pull the boat off, in effect, by its own bootstraps.

Saltwater sailors have one additional problem to worry about when running aground: the tide. A boat grounded at low tide will often float free without any fuss when the water level rises with the incoming tide. But if the tide is going out, the vessel may be stranded until the next high tide. Unless the boat is light enough to be dragged to deep water, there is no cure for this misfortune except to sit patiently and vow to remember the old seamen's warning: "Never go aground on an ebb tide."

Perils of Inlets

In the normal course of boat handling, nothing is more consistently hazardous than running an inlet such as the one shown here, the narrow and often treacherous gateway connecting the Atlantic Ocean with Barnegat Bay on the New Jersey coast. On the Atlantic and Gulf littorals, hundreds of such inlets confront the seafarer with churning, shallow waters, rip tides and other hazards. These phenomena are duplicated—and sometimes surpassed—on the Pacific coast at the mouths of such big rivers as the Columbia, whose waters flow into the ocean over a two-mile stretch of shallow sand bars, rocks, sunken logs and jetsam. In 1973, the U.S. Coast Guard plucked 39 people from the mouth of the Columbia and went to the aid of 720 disabled boats in those troubled waters.

What makes inlets so formidable is that the waves sweeping in on a shoaling coast are funneled by an inlet's entrance and heaved up into steep, cresting walls of water. These are especially dangerous when an onshore wind drives them against a tidal current pouring out of the inlet. Trouble in such turbulent conditions comes most often on the inbound passage, because an overtaking sea is usually more dangerous than a wave that is encountered head on. Moreover, a skipper on the inside can simply decide not to go out, whereas one on the outside not only is anxious to get home but also, being behind the waves, is often unable to tell how bad the inlet is until he's in it.

Before making the plunge, a good seaman takes some precautions. He moves passengers and gear aft so that the bow of his boat will be light enough to avoid being buried in a wave. He makes sure all watertight compartments are properly sealed. In rough seas he tells all hands to put on life jackets. And if conditions look really bad, the skipper simply waits outside for the turn of the tide—the moment when seas around an inlet are smoothest.

Once committed to run an inlet, the skipper's most urgent concern is to keep the boat lined up perpendicular to the waves so as not to broach, or swing broadside, into a position where the boat could be swamped or swept out of the channel onto rocks or a sand bar. To avoid such a calamity, the pilot must keep a constant watch both ahead and astern. He must time his run and place his boat so that either the waves pass him safely by, or as the outboard shown above is doing, the boat rides the back of a cresting wave all the way to calm water.

Safely steering a 17-foot outboard runabout through Barnegat Inlet, the skipper above has his boat under firm control, positioned at a perpendicular angle to the waves, bow up and short of the crest. In this case he matches the boat's speed to the wave's, throttling up to hold his position just behind the crest. But if the surf should be moving faster than his boat, he would slow down each time an overtaking wave lifted his stern to keep the bow from driving into the trough. Either way, he keeps his stern dead on to the waves.

Risking trouble, the pilot at left is pushing the bow of the boat through the crest of a wave into a dangerous attitude from which the craft could slide down the face of the breaker and become swamped or overturned. The safest procedure in this instance is to throttle down a little and then hold a position in the safe zone behind the whitecap.

Towing in Tandem

Towing may sometimes be a matter of convenience rather than emergency, as when a powerboat like the one at right tows a string of sailboats to the starting line for a race or back again after the finish. This time-saving procedure requires a special arrangement of the towing lines and a vigilant, capable helmsman in every boat of the cavalcade.

The towline from the powerboat is secured with a loop, or eye, around the mast of the first boat. A line from the second boat is tied into the same loop, on the after side of the mast. This second line runs the length of the first boat and the other end of this line is looped around the second boat's mast. The third boat is attached to the second boat in exactly the same way, and so on down the line. With this arrangement, the towing load is taken mostly by the towlines and not by any fittings on the boats that might not be up to the strain.

The powerboat should proceed at a slow, steady rate. Too much speed will send the small boats slewing around from side to side. Some experienced seamen feel that two shorter lines of boats—one from each quarter of the towboat—are easier for the towboat to handle than one long line. On the other hand, this setup requires more precise steering in each of the towed boats, because the two lines will have a tendency to come together.

In any case, the towed sailors must keep alert throughout the maneuver—one boat swerving out of line can throw the whole flotilla into confusion.

A launch tows 10 small sailboats to port after a day's racing. The first dinghy is pulled by a line to the powerboat's stern; each following boat rides on a line from its mast to that of the boat in front, at an interval of 10 to 15 feet. The lifejacketed sailors (all but one incautious boatman) stay low in their vessels, steering a steady course.

Locking Through

Anyone who cruises within the 30,000-mile network of the United States inland waterways will sooner or later encounter a lock, a device for passing boats between a lower and a higher body of water. The lock chamber is closed at each end by gates. Valves let water flow in from the higher body to lock boats up, and drain out to the lower body to lock them down.

Locking through, the process shown here, is easy enough with careful use of the right equipment and a knowledge of locking procedures. Like towing, locking through requires plenty of lines and fenders. Two of the lines should be at least as long as the depth of the deepest lock to be transited, to moor bow and stern to the lock wall. Better still are lines twice the deepest lock depth. A line that long, passed around a mooring post or bollard on the lock wall and back to the deck, can be cast off and pulled back around the bollard to the boat without help from shore. Thrifty boatmen use old or cheap rope for lock lines since they quickly become chafed and dirty. Fenders used alone or supplemented with boards hung outside them protect a boat's sides from scraping the walls and from banging into other boats tied up alongside.

On approaching most locks, a boatman must give specific sound or radio signals. These vary considerably across the country and even between locks in the same system. By consulting charts or a nearby marina operator, a yachtsman can learn what signal is expected of him. Usually he must await a reply from the lock master, who may have to give priority to military and commercial craft.

A skipper given clearance enters the lock slowly and ties up as directed by a lock attendant who may provide the docking lines, or lower a light line with which to haul up the boat's locking line. If not, the boatman must heave his line up to the attendant. Lines must be carefully tended to keep the boat from drifting or, during locking up, from being tossed about by turbulent water near the inlet valve. A boat locking down must have its lines payed out as the level drops, to avert the chagrin—and possible serious damage—arising from hanging a boat up on a bollard. This peril is avoided in locks that have camels—floating mooring docks that rise and fall with the water level.

When the lock gates open, the boatmen cast off at the lock master's signal and depart slowly in the order of entry, making as little wake as possible and avoiding the prop wash from large vessels.

The first of a line of boats comes slowly into a lock, with fenders out, and takes its place at the head of the lock, directed by attendants atop the lock wall. The line tender in the bow waits for the lock attendant to slip the loop in the end of the line over a bollard before taking up the slack. The attendant standing above the stern will do the same with a line passed to him by the man in the stern. Both line tenders aboard the boat will lead their lines through chocks and ease the boat up to the lock wall by hauling together. They will stay on station all during the procedure, to take in their lines as necessary.

While line tenders hold the first boat steady against the lock wall, a second boat approaches with fenders out and prepares to tie up to the first. More boats will follow, but since they will all rise together, the lines from boat to boat do not have to be tended continuously.

As the lock fills with water, the boats rise with it to the top of the wall. Bow and stern locking lines have been hauled in to keep them taut. Now the lock gates will open, and at a signal from the lock master the boats will slowly depart, the inside boat leaving first.

On a sunny summer afternoon, the 825-foot-long Hiram M. Chittenden lock, near Seattle, Washington, looks like an urban throughway at rush hour as boatmen crowd into it after a day on Puget Sound. But if fenders are in place, line tenders alert and helmsmen patient, all the craft in this waterborne traffic jam will soon get safely lifted about 10 feet to the level of Lake Washington and be on their way home.

A Gazetteer to the Rules of the Road

The maps on these pages define the waters in and around the United States to which the four basic sets of navigation rules (pp. 104-125) apply. The first of these regulations were framed in 1864 as an increasing volume of commerce moved up the Mississippi River, and they evolved into the Western Rivers Rules. The Great Lakes Rules were drawn in 1895, and in 1897 came the Inland Rules, which apply to all other inland waters. Inland Rules also cover some specifically designated coastal areas, and all coastal waters inside a line drawn through the outermost buoys marking bays, sounds and other estuaries. On unmarked coasts, and on the high seas, International Rules apply.

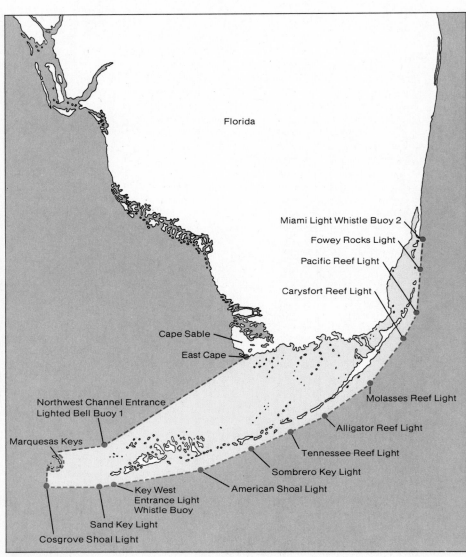

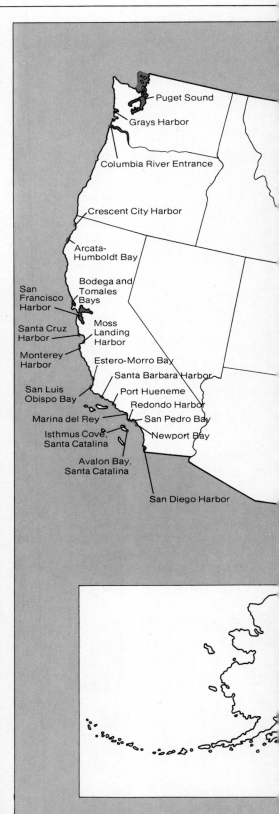

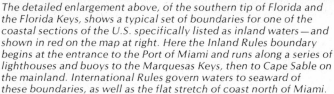

The detailed enlargement above, of the southern tip of Florida and the Florida Keys, shows a typical set of boundaries for one of the coastal sections of the U.S. specifically listed as inland waters—and shown in red on the map at right. Here the Inland Rules boundary begins at the entrance to the Port of Miami and runs along a series of lighthouses and buoys to the Marquesas Keys, then to Cape Sable on the mainland. International Rules govern waters to seaward of these boundaries, as well as the flat stretch of coast north of Miami.

Red River of the North

Great Lakes

West Quoddy Head

Cape Ann

Massachusetts Bay

Nantucket Sound

Long Island Sound

New York Harbor

Delaware Bay

Chesapeake Bay

Atlantic Ocean

Mississippi River

Charleston Harbor

Savannah Harbor

St. Simons,
St. Andrews and Cumberland Sounds

St. Johns River

Atchafalaya River

Apalachee Bay

Mobile Bay

Galveston Bay

Mississippi Delta

Tampa Bay

Charlotte Harbor

San Carlos Bay

Rio Grande

Florida Keys

Inland Rules

Great Lakes Rules

Gulf of Mexico

Western Rivers Rules

Hawaii

Mamala Bay

encer

In this map, waters covered by Western Rivers Rules are shown in blue; they include the Mississippi (except for the delta below New Orleans) and its tributaries, the Red River of the North and part of the Atchafalaya River. Great Lakes Rules cover the five lakes and tributaries—colored green—east to Montreal. Shown in red are the coastal areas of the United States specifically designated as inland waters. The smaller of these are identified above by name, the larger ones by the geographical features that mark their outer limits.

A Summary of Federal Boating Rules

The chart below sums up federal regulations governing the equipment required on pleasure boats up to 65 feet, as well as rules on registration, accidents and water pollution. (Owners of yachts larger than 65 feet should consult the Coast Guard about equipment regulations.) The rules for running lights are on pages 116-125. Boatmen should also investigate state and local laws in their areas; handbooks on state laws are available from the Outdoor Boating Club, 401 North Michigan Avenue, Chicago, Illinois, 60611.

Equipment Required	Class A Less than 16 feet	Class 1 16 to less than 26 feet	Class 2 26 to less than 40 feet	Class 3 40 to not more than 65 feet
Whistle or horn	None required; but Rules of the Road demand some audible signaling device	Whistle or horn, operated by hand, mouth or power and audible for at least one half mile	Whistle or horn, operated by hand or power and audible for at least one mile	Whistle or horn, operated by power and audible for at least one mile
Bell	None required		One that produces "a clear bell-like tone"	
Fire extinguishers: For boats with no fixed system installed	On boats of closed construction, at least one two-pound dry chemical or one four-pound CO_2 extinguisher. None required on completely open boats. *Note: The extinguishers listed here refer to Coast Guard-approved portable dry chemical or CO_2 types; for other types, in less general use, see pages 16-17.*		At least one 10-pound or two two-pound dry chemical extinguishers; or one 15-pound or two four-pound CO_2 extinguishers	One two-pound plus one 10-pound, or three two-pound dry chemical extinguishers; or three four-pound or one four-pound plus one 15-pound CO_2 extinguishers
For boats with automatic or remotely controlled system	No portable extinguishers required		At least one two-pound dry chemical or one four-pound CO_2 portable extinguisher	One 10-pound or two two-pound dry chemical extinguishers; or one 15-pound or two four-pound CO_2 portable extinguishers
Flotation devices	One Type I, II, III or IV for each person	One wearable device (Type I, II or III) readily accessible for each person aboard or water skiing, plus one Type IV throwable device at hand *Note: Reference is to Coast Guard-approved personal flotation devices (pages 16-17), which must be legibly tagged to indicate type.*		
Flame arrester	One on each carburetor of gasoline engines installed after April 25, 1940 (except for outboard motors)			
Ventilation	On boats built or decked over since April 25, 1940 (except those using diesel fuel), at least two ventilator ducts with cowls for properly airing the bilges or any other compartment which can trap gas vapors.			

Registration, identification numbers and documentation	Under Federal law, all motor-equipped boats, except those used only for racing, must be registered or documented and must display an identification number. State agencies register boats except in Alaska, New Hampshire, Washington and the District of Columbia, where they are registered by the Coast Guard. The identification number must appear on each side of the bow in letters at least three inches tall. (Tenders of yachts registered by the Coast Guard use the parent boat's number plus the suffix "1" and are not registered separately.) Any boat built since November 1, 1972 will also have a hull identification number, permanently mounted by the builder in letters at least one quarter inch high on the outboard side of	the transom or the starboard side of the hull. All boats less than 20 feet long (except canoes, kayaks, inflatables and motorless sailboats) built since November 1, 1972 must also display a plaque noting the engine's horsepower and the weight the boat can safely carry. The state agency or the Coast Guard must be notified within 15 days if a boat is stolen, sold or abandoned. If the boat is moved to another state it must be re-registered within 60 days. Instead of paying for registration, the owner of a craft larger than about 30 feet may ask the Coast Guard to document his vessel, a free service that provides a permanent record of the ship's papers and facilitates the subsequent sale, charter or mortgage of the vessel.
Accident responsibility	Any skipper involved in an accident must first help any injured person. He must also give his name, address and boat registration number to every injured person or owner of damaged property. The state agency or the Coast Guard must be notified within 48 hours of an	accident in which a person is disabled for more than 24 hours, dies within 24 hours of the accident, or disappears from the boat under circumstances that indicate death or injury. Accidents in which property damage exceeds $100 must be reported in five days.
Water pollution	Federal law forbids the pumping of oil or oily wastes into navigable U.S. waters or even into a boat's bilge. The law also requires the conspicuous display of a sign	to this effect in any boat over 26 feet long. Such signs, and instructions for where to post them, are available free from most marine insurance companies.

Glossary

Aback A sail is aback when it is trimmed to windward. *(See Back.)*

Abeam A direction at right angles to the centerline of the boat.

Aft Toward the stern.

Amidships In or near the middle of a boat, either along the longitudinal axis or from side to side.

Apparent wind The wind that blows across a boat, composed of a combination of true wind and wind created by the boat's forward motion.

Back To back a sail is to trim it to windward. A sail backs, or is taken aback, if it is left cleated too long during a tack, or if a wind shift brings the wind to the other side of the bow. Jibs are often purposely backed when the skipper wants to sail backward, either to get out of irons or to leave a mooring or dock.

Backwater To move a rowboat backward by pushing the oars so that the oar blades move through the water from aft forward.

Backwind Wind deflected from one sail onto the leeward side of another, or deflected from the sails of one boat onto those of a boat astern.

Battens Flexible strips of wood or fiberglass placed in a sail to help the leech retain its proper shape.

Bear off To turn a boat away from the direction of the wind.

Beat To go to windward in a sailboat by sailing alternate legs, with the wind first on one side and then on the other.

Block A wood or metal shell that encloses one or more sheaves, or pulleys, through which lines are led.

Bollard A strong metal or wood post on a pier or towboat used to secure docking and towing lines.

Boltrope A rope sewed to the luff or foot of a sail to strengthen it against tearing.

Boom vang A single wire or a block and tackle commonly used to hold down the boom while reaching or running.

Broach To swing out of control when running so that the boat turns beam on to wind and sea, in danger of capsizing.

Burdened vessel Under the Rules of the Road, the vessel which does not have right of way and which must take action to avoid collision.

By the lee A condition that occurs during downwind sailing, when the wind comes over the side of the boat on which the sail is set.

Cam cleat A quick-release cleat having two side-by-side, spring-loaded cams with teeth. A line leading between the cams is held in the teeth but can be released by a quick upward pull on the line.

Catch a crab When rowing, to accidentally catch an oar blade so that it buries underwater instead of lifting free.

Centerboard A plate of wood or metal, hinged on a pin and lowered into the water through a watertight housing, or trunk. A centerboard resists the tendency of a sailboat to slide sideways when sailing.

Chain plate A long, narrow metal plate attached to the side of the hull as a fastening point for shrouds and stays.

Chock A metal fitting, usually mounted on or in a boat's rail, to guide hawsers or ropes for mooring or towing.

Claw off To beat to windward off a lee shore.

Cleat A wood or metal fitting with two projecting horns, fastened to some part of the boat, to which a line is belayed.

Clevis pin A small cylindrically shaped pin used to close shackles or outhaul fittings, or to fasten a turnbuckle to a chain plate.

Clew The lower, after corner of a sail, where the foot meets the leech.

Close-hauled A boat is said to be close-hauled when it is sailing close to the wind (about 45° off the wind) and its sails are trimmed in tight.

Coaming A raised framing around deck openings such as hatches or cockpits to keep water out.

Cockpit A well in the deck, usually aft, where a boat's wheel or tiller is located.

Come about To steer a sailboat through the eye of the wind so that the sails shift from one side of the boat to the other, putting the boat on another tack.

Coupler A device for attaching a trailer to a towing vehicle's hitch.

Cringle A circular eye, often formed by a metal ring or grommet, set in the corners or on the edges of a sail and used for fastening the sail to spars or running rigging.

Cuddy A small enclosed space or cabin in a small boat.

Day shape A distinctive object, such as a sphere or cylinder displayed in a ship's rigging, during daylight hours, to indicate a particular status with respect to the Rules of the Road.

Dinghy A small rowboat, often a tender to a larger boat. Also, any small sailboat.

Downhaul The wire or rope tackle that pulls down the foremost end of the boom so as to tighten the luff of a sail.

Down The direction away from the wind; to leeward.

Draft The depth a vessel extends below the waterline.

Engine brace A device used to support an outboard engine on the transom of a boat being trailered.

Fairlead A metal or wooden eye that guides a rope in a desired direction.

Fall off To steer a boat away from the direction of the wind.

Feather To turn an oar blade after the pulling stroke so that it rests or moves nearly parallel to the water, and offers the least possible resistance to wind and waves.

Foot Bottom edge of a sail.

Fore and aft A boat's longitudinal axis.

Foreguy A line running from the outboard end of a spinnaker pole to a block on the foredeck, used to keep the end of the spinnaker pole from rising.

Genoa A large headsail set on the headstay and overlapping the mainsail.

Gooseneck The fitting, connecting mast and boom, that allows the boom to swing laterally and vertically.

Gudgeon One of a pair of sockets into which pins called pintles are fitted to attach the rudder to the boat.

Gunwale The rail of a boat. (Pronounced GUN-nel.)

Guy The name for the spinnaker sheet that is to windward, used to control the spinnaker pole.

Guy hook A fitting, placed on the deck of some small boats, through which the guy is led to counteract the spinnaker pole's tendency to ride up in the air.

Halyard A line used either to hoist or lower a sail.

Hank A fitting used to attach the luff of the jib to the headstay.

Head The top corner of a triangular sail. Also, a seagoing lavatory.

Head down To steer a boat away from the direction of the wind.

Head up To steer a boat closer to the direction from which the wind is coming.

Header A shift in the wind's direction toward a boat's bow, forcing the boat to head down or the crew to trim sail.

Hike out To sit on the windward rail and lean out over the water to counteract the boat's tendency to heel.

Hiking stick A right-angle extension of the tiller that enables the helmsman to hike out and still manage the tiller.

Hitch ball An attachment put on a car to receive a trailer's coupler.

Hound A band near the top of the mast with eyes for securing the tops of shrouds and stays.

Hourglass A fouled spinnaker whose middle is twisted so that the wind fills only the top and the bottom of the sail.

Irons A sailboat is said to be in irons when it is pointed directly into the wind without steerageway.

Jib A triangular sail set on a headstay.

Jibe To turn a boat's stern through the wind so that the sails swing from one side of the boat to the other, putting the boat on another tack.

Kedge A small anchor. Also, as a verb, to move a boat through the water by putting out an anchor and then pulling in on the anchor rode.

Leech The after edge of a sail.

Leeward In the direction away from the wind. (Pronounced LOO-ard.)

Leeway Drift, or sideways slip of a boat, due to the pressure of wind on the sails.

Lift A shift in the wind's direction away from a boat's bow, allowing a sailboat to point higher than it could previously.

Line Nautical usage for rope used aboard a boat.

Luff The leading edge of the sail. Also, the fluttering of a sail when the boat is pointed too close to the wind, or the sail is let out too far.

Mast step Socket in which the heel, or bottom, of a mast is stepped.

Masthead fly A wind indicator mounted on top of a mast.

Miss stays To fail to bring a boat through the wind when coming about and to fall back on the former tack.

Oarlocks Swiveling devices fitted into a rowboat's gunwales to serve as pivot points for the oars.

Off the wind In a direction other than close-hauled, e.g. a reach or a run.

Outhaul A fitting on the boom to which the sail's clew is attached, and by means of which the foot of the sail is stretched out along the boom.

Painter A bow line for a small boat.

Pintle A pin that fits into a gudgeon to attach the rudder to the boat.

Point To sail close to the wind. Also, one of 32 divisions on the compass, each equal to 11¼.°

Port The left side of a boat, when looking forward.

Pram A small rowboat or sailing dinghy with a squared-off bow.

Primer bulb A rubber bulb in an outboard's gas line; when squeezed and released, the bulb sucks gas out of the tank and into the line.

Privileged vessel The boat which has the right of way under the Rules of the Road, and must maintain its course and speed.

Quarter Either side of a boat's stern.

Reach A course sailed between a beat and a run, with the wind coming more or less at right angles over a boat's side. On a close reach the wind is farther forward; on a broad reach, farther aft.

Reef To reduce the area of a sail by lowering it somewhat and tying down its foot.

Rig A noun indicating the arrangement of masts, rigging and sails by which a vessel is distinguished, as a ketch or a yawl, etc. Also, a verb meaning to prepare a boat or some piece of nautical gear for service.

Rigging The lines or wires fitted to spars and sails for support and control. Standing rigging is made up of the fixed shrouds and stays that provide lateral and longitudinal support to the spars. Running rigging comprises the halyards, sheets, tackles, outhauls and downhauls to put up, take down and adjust sails.

Right-handed propeller A propeller whose blades, viewed from aft when the boat is going ahead, turn clockwise. Most outboards and single-engine inboards have right-handed propellers.

Roach The area at the after edge of a sail between its leech and a straight line drawn from head to clew.

Rode An anchor line.

Run To sail before the wind. Also the narrowing part of the hull, aft, underwater.

Running lights Navigation lights required by rules of the nautical road in different combinations for different sizes and types of vessel. Usually they consist of a red light to port and green to starboard, plus one or more white lights.

Scull To swing an oar back and forth through the water off the stern of a boat so that the boat moves forward. Also, to move a tiller rapidly back and forth, thus propelling the boat forward.

Shackle A U-shaped metal fitting with a cross pin or clevis pin that fits across the opening of the U as a closure.

Sheave The grooved wheel in a block, or in a masthead fitting or elsewhere, over which a rope runs. (Pronounced shiv.)

Sheet A line used to trim a sail.

Shell A long, light craft in which oarsmen row competitively.

Ship oars To take the oars out of the oarlocks and lay them in the boat.

Shrouds Ropes or wires, led from the mast to the chain plates at deck level on either side of the mast, which keep it from falling sideways.

Sideslip To be pushed sideways through the water by the wind; to make leeway.

Skeg A fixed triangular fin extending down under the stern of a small boat and aiding the boat to follow a straight course.

Slip A narrow berth for a boat, either at a pier or dock.

Spar General term for any wood or metal pole—mast, boom, yard, gaff or sprit—used to carry and give shape to sails.

Spinnaker A full-bellied, lightweight sail set forward of the mast on a spinnaker pole and carried when a sailboat is reaching or running.

Spreaders Pairs of horizontal struts attached to each side of the mast and used to hold the shrouds away from the mast, thus giving them a wider purchase.

Starboard The right side of a boat, looking forward.

Starter solenoid A relay switch that, when activated by pushing the starter button, conducts power from the battery to the starter motor.

Stay A rope or wire running forward or aft from the mast to support it.

Stretcher A footboard against which an oarsman braces his feet in a rowboat.

Surge brakes Brakes on a trailer that operate automatically when momentum causes a trailer to surge forward against its towing hitch.

Tack A noun indicating the lower forward corner of a sail. Also, a noun indicating which side of a vessel the wind is coming over, i.e., a boat is on the port tack if the wind comes over its port side. Also as a verb, to alter a boat's course through the eye of the wind so that the wind blows on the other side of the boat. *(See Come about.)*

Tabling Reinforcement around the edges of a sail made by hemming the sailcloth.

Tang A metal fitting on a mast to which the top of a shroud or stay is attached.

Telltale A piece of yarn tied to shrouds or sails to indicate the direction of the wind.

Thole pins Wood or metal pins fitted into a rowboat's gunwales to serve the same purpose as oarlocks.

Thwart A crosswise seat in an open boat.

Tie-down A wire or fabric strap that secures a boat to its trailer.

Tiller An arm, or lever, connected to the rudder for steering.

Tilt pin A metal pin that keeps the tilting frame of a tilt-bed trailer in place until the boat is ready for launching.

Topping lift A halyard attached to the spinnaker pole, and raised or lowered to keep the spinnaker properly trimmed. Also, a line from the masthead to the end of the main boom to hold up the boom when no sail is set.

Topsides The sides of the boat from waterline to rail.

Transom The aftermost part of the stern, usually bearing the boat's name.

Trim To adjust the set of a sail relative to the wind. Also to adjust a boat's load so that the craft rides at the desired attitude.

Trim tabs Hinged plates attached to the transom of a powerboat to keep the stern from burying when the boat is run at high speeds.

Turnbuckle An adjustable fastening for attaching the standing rigging to the chain plates.

Twin screw Having two propellers—usually one right-handed, one left-handed.

Underway Generally, moving through the water; specifically under the Rules of the Road, to be not at anchor or otherwise made fast to the shore or ground—though not necessarily moving forward.

Up In a sailboat, the direction toward the wind. To head up is to turn a boat to windward.

Wetted surface The immersed area of a floating hull.

Whistle signal A sound produced by a horn, whistle or similar device, and used to indicate either the presence of a vessel in reduced visibility or the intention of a vessel in a right of way situation. The whistle signals required by the Rules of the Road are described in blasts; a short blast is a blast of about 1 second in duration, a prolonged blast, 4 to 6 seconds, a long blast 8 to 10 seconds.

Winch A device with a revolving drum, around which a line may be turned in order to provide mechanical advantage in hoisting or hauling.

Windmill While rowing, to raise the oars too high out of the water and then bury them too deeply.

Windward The direction toward the wind source.

Yaw The side-to-side deviation of a boat from its course caused by bad steering or by heavy seas.

Bibliography

General

Allen, Jim J., *Boating*. The Ronald Press Co., 1958.

Blanchard, Fessenden S., and William T. Stone, *A Cruising Guide to the Chesapeake*. Dodd, Mead & Co., 1968.

Bolger, Philip C., *Small Boats*. International Marine Publishing Company, 1973.

Bottomley, Tom, *The Complete Book of Boat Trailering*. Association Press, 1974.

Chapman, Charles Frederic, *Piloting, Seamanship and Small Boat Handling*. Motor Boating & Sailing Books, The Hearst Corporation, 1974.

Cotter, Edward F., *Multihull Sailboats*. Crown Publishers, Inc., 1971.

Federal Requirements for Recreational Boats. U.S. Coast Guard Publication CG-290. U.S. Government Printing Office, 1974.

Henderson, Richard:
Sail and Power. Naval Institute Press, 1973.
Sea Sense. International Marine Publishing Co., 1972.

Herreshoff, L. Francis, *The Compleat Cruiser*. Sheridan House, 1972.

Hiscock, Eric C., *Cruising Under Sail*. Oxford University Press, 1972.

Hoyt, Norris D., *Seamanship*. The Dial Press, 1960.

Jones, Ted, *The Offshore Racer*, Quadrangle/The New York Times Book Co., 1973.

Kals, W. S., *Practical Boating*. Doubleday & Company, Inc., 1969.

Kenealy, James P., *Boating from Bow to Stern*. Hawthorn Books, Inc., 1966.

Lee, E.C.B., and Kenneth Lee, *Safety and Survival at Sea*. A Giniger Book published in association with W. W. Norton & Company, 1972.

Liebers, Arthur, *Encyclopedia of Pleasure Boating*. A. S. Barnes and Company, Inc., 1961.

Street, Donald M., Jr., *The Ocean Sailing Yacht*. W. W. Norton & Company, Inc., 1973.

Walliser, Blair, *Basic Seamanship and Safe Boat Handling*. Doubleday & Company, Inc., 1972.

Weeks, Morris, Jr., ed., *The Complete Boating Encyclopedia*. The Odyssey Press, 1964.

Zadig, Ernest A., *The Complete Book of Boating*. Prentice-Hall, Inc., 1972.

Powerboating

Anderson, Edwin P., *Audels Outboard Motor and Boating Guide*. Theo. Audel & Co., 1963.

Smith, Geoffrey, *Power Boating*. Wilfred Funk Inc., 1955.

Watson, Ted, *Handling Small Boats Under Power*. Adlard Coles, Ltd., 1971.

West, Jack, *Modern Powerboats*. Van Nostrand Reinhold Company, 1970.

Sailboat Handling

Bavier, Robert N., Jr., *Sailing to Win*. Dodd, Mead & Company, 1969.

Colgate, Stephen, *Colgate's Basic Sailing Theory*. Van Nostrand Reinhold Company, 1973.

Creagh-Osborne, Richard, *This Is Sailing*. Sail Books, Inc., 1973.

Farnham, Moulton H., *Sailing for Beginners*. Macmillan Publishing Co., Inc., 1971.

Gibbs, Tony, *Practical Sailing*. Motor Boating & Sailing Books, The Hearst Corporation, 1971.

Smith, Hervey Garrett, *The Small-Boat Sailor's Bible*. Doubleday & Company, Inc., 1974.

White, Reg, and Bob Fisher, *Catamaran Racing*. John de Graff Inc., 1973.

Wilson, Chris, and Max Press, *Catamaran Sailing to Win*. A. S. Barnes & Co., 1973.

Rules of the Road

Hilbert, William Edward, *The International Rules of the Road at Sea*. Dissertation to Georgetown Law Faculty, 1938.

Prunski, Alfred, ed., *Farwell's Rules of the Nautical Road*. Revised edition. United States Naval Institute, 1971.

Rules of the Road, Great Lakes, U.S. Coast Guard Publication CG-172. U.S. Government Printing Office, 1966.

Rules of the Road, International-Inland, U.S. Coast Guard Publication CG-169. U.S. Government Printing Office, 1972.

Rules of the Road, Western Rivers, U.S. Coast Guard Publication CG-184. U.S. Government Printing Office, 1972.

Histories

Ashburner, Walter, ed., *The Rhodian Sea-Law*. Clarendon Press, 1909.

Grenfell, Captain Russell, R.N., *Nelson the Sailor*. The Macmillan Company, 1950.

Hoyt, C. Sherman, *Memoirs*. D. Van Nostrand Company, Inc., 1950.

Loomis, Alfred F., *Ocean Racing: 1866-1935*. Arno Press, 1967.

Oman, Carola, *Nelson*. Doubleday & Company, Inc., 1946.

Warner, Oliver, *A Portrait of Lord Nelson*. Penguin Books, Ltd., 1963.

Rowing

Emmett, Jim A.:
"Art of Rowing." *Outdoor Life*, May, 1960, pp. 136-138.
"The Lost Art of Sculling." *Mechanix Illustrated*, February, 1969, pp. 80, 131-132.

Kelley, Robert F., *American Rowing*. G. P. Putnam's Sons, 1932.

Paulson, F. M., "The Rewards of Rowing," *Field & Stream*, July, 1968, pp. 92-96.

Boating Courses

A prudent step between reading about boating and going afloat is taking a course in boat handling, seamanship and safety. Hundreds of local schools and clubs schedule private classes in all facets of boating. The national organizations listed below provide curricula free or at little cost. Many state and city recreation departments also sponsor public courses.

1. U.S. Power Squadrons. More than 400 local units of this national organization of recreational boatmen present free to the public a 10-lesson course in basic boating safety at least once a year. To its members, the USPS also offers advanced instruction on seamanship and navigation. For information, call your local unit, or national headquarters in Mondale, New Jersey, toll free, (800) 243-6000.

2. The U.S. Coast Guard. For those who live where other general courses are unavailable, the Coast Guard offers a correspondence "Skipper's Course." Write to the Office of Boating Safety, 400 Seventh Street, SW, Washington, D.C. 20590.

3. The Coast Guard Auxiliary. A volunteer civilian arm of the service, the auxiliary sponsors a number of courses in boating safety for the public. Call one of the 18 district offices or your local group.

4. The American Red Cross. Many local Red Cross chapters periodically conduct small-boat safety classes designed by the national organization.

Acknowledgments

Portions of *Boat Handling* were written by Reginald Bragonier Jr., Timothy Foote, Peter Stoller, Peter Swerdloff and Keith Wheeler. For help given in the preparation of this book, the editors also wish to thank: Henry Anderson, North American Yacht Racing Union, New York, New York; Bill Aucoin, Johnson Motors, Waukegan, Illinois; Richard D. Boger, Norwalk Cove Marina, Inc., East Norwalk, Connecticut; Stephen Colgate, New York, New York; Joseph Cruz, Hempstead, New York; Michael J. Dapice, Aeronautical, Inc., Greenwich, Connecticut; Ronald J. Dittmar, The Shipyard, Clayton, New York; Petty Officer Dennis Florence, U.S. Coast Guard, Brooklyn, New York; Frank Futie, Aeronautical, Inc., Greenwich, Connecticut; Robert A. Gilchrist, Controller, E-Z Loader Boat Trailers, Spokane, Washington; Harold Grossman, Holsclaw Bros., Evansville, Indiana; Lee F. Hartog, Rowayton Marine Works, Inc., Rowayton, Connecticut; Bolling W. Haxall, Clayton, New York; Howard K. Hayden, Long Branch, New Jersey; Lawrence N. Johnson, President, E-Z Loader Boat Trailers, Spokane, Washington; John R. Kellogg, The Shipyard, Clayton, New York; Robert V. Lashomb, The Shipyard, Clayton, New York; Robert A. Massey, Navesink Yacht Sales, Inc., Sea Bright, New Jersey; Chief Thomas McAdams, U.S. Coast Guard, Newport, Oregon; John H. Page, Huntington, New York; C. E. Parson, Glastron Boat Company, Austin, Texas; Carol Patrick, North American Sailing Association, Newport Beach, California; Graeme Paxton, Evinrude, Milwaukee, Wisconsin; Ralph Poole, Editor and Publisher, *Trailer Boats Magazine*, Burbank, California; Lt.(jg) F. J. Sambor, U.S. Coast Guard, Governors Island, New York; Captain E. Arthur Shuman Jr., U.S. Navy (ret), Stuart, Florida; Francis J. Silva, President, Bryan Metal Products, Inc., Middletown, Connecticut; Frank Smith and Ronald Smith, Smitty's Marine Inc., Lake Hopatcong, New Jersey; Kenneth F. Stirlitz, Orlando Power Squadron, Maitland, Florida; Miles Suchomel, Underwriters' Laboratories, Northbrook, Illinois; Rick Taylor, Costa Mesa, California; K. E. Wadman, Commander, U.S. Coast Guard, Washington, D.C.; John Wisdom, Bertram Yacht Co., New York, New York; Glen L. Witt, Glen Marine Designs, Bellflower, California; William Ziegler III, Darien, Connecticut.

Picture Credits
Credits from left to right are separated by semicolons, from top to bottom by dashes.

Cover—Eric Schweikardt. 6, 7—Chris Caswell. 9—Sebastian Milito. 12—Ken Kay. 14 through 29—Drawings by Fred Wolff. 19—Starter Solenoid drawing courtesy Outboard Marine Corporation. 30, 31 —Drawings by Hugh Chevins. 32 through 37—Ken Kay, drawings by Hugh Chevins. 38, 39—Culver Pictures. 40, 41—South Street Seaport Museum. 42, 43—Official United States Navy photo; Alice Austen, courtesy Staten Island Historical Society. 44, 45—Peabody Museum of Salem; Thousand Islands Museum. 46, 47—Howard K. Hayden. 48—Stephen Green-Armytage. 50, 51—Drawings by Nicholas Fasciano. 52, 53—Stephen Green-Armytage, drawings by Nicholas Fasciano. 54, 55 —Stephen Green-Armytage, drawings by Nicholas Fasciano adapted from Stephen Green-Armytage photos. 56 through 61 —Stephen Green-Armytage, drawings by Nicholas Fasciano. 62 through 67 —George Silk from TIME-LIFE Picture Agency. 68—Thomas Zimmerman from Alpha Photo Associates. 70 through 93 —Drawings by Don Bolognese. 94 through 103—Eric Schweikardt. 104—Stephen Green-Armytage. 106 through 125 —Drawings by Dale Gustafson. 126 —John Zimmerman. 128 through 133 —Drawings by William G. Teodecki. 134 through 139—Al Freni. 140, 141—Drawings by William G. Teodecki. 142, 143 —Ralph Poole from *Trailer Boats Magazine*. 144 through 159—Stephen Green-Armytage, drawings on 148 and 153 by Gerhard Richter adapted from Stephen Green-Armytage photos. 160, 161—Enrico Ferorelli. 162 through 165—Steve Wilson. 166, 167—Maps by Nicholas Fasciano.

Index *Page numbers in italics indicate illustrations*